TEACHING TACTICS

for Japan's English Classrooms

John Wharton

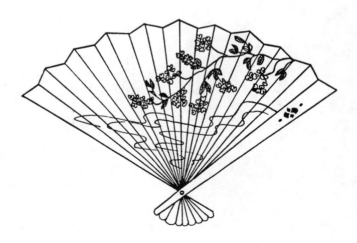

Please address correspondence and orders for additional copies (US$6.95 each, fourth-class postage included) to:

The Global Press
1510 York St., Suite 204
Denver, Colorado 80206 USA

ISBN 0-011285-02-4

Printed in the United States of America

First Edition

Contents

Introduction

There are those (some Japanese, mostly native speakers) who say there's something slightly unseemly about a person teaching English who gained the gift of that valuable language by dint of birth rather than struggle. And I think all English as a Second Language teachers have wrestled with some small bit of--what, guilt?--at how very well we effortlessly speak the language and how abysmally most Japanese students handle it, even after a decade of hard study.

But such is the situation in Nippon and the sad fact is that English is one tough nut to crack, especially when the cracker comes from a linguistic background as alien as Japanese. Sure we native-speakers are darned lucky to have been born in a land where English is the dominant language but that's Lady Luck for you.

But, of course, such "luck" works both ways. If and when you hear a student bemoaning his misfortune at not having been born to English, remind him that there are plenty of "gaijin" (foreigners) trying to learn to speak Japanese as well as he can without giving it a second thought!

Still, there's just no comparison between the numbers of people learning English and those learning any other language on the planet. You, as a native English speaker, blessed with the world language as your mother tongue, are just what the millions and millions of Japanese students of our language think they need to "internationalize" (*the* current buzzword of choice in Japan). And, as you've probably learned either first-hand, from friends or from my guidebook, <u>JOBS IN JAPAN</u>, the Japanese are very eager to have you teach them what you (luckily) never had to learn.

Easy money? Well, although the pay can be very good for English teachers in Japan (ranging to $60 an hour just to chat with a businessman), most of the work requires preparation, extreme concentration and just plain energy. You'll earn every yen you make in the classroom, believe me!

I'm often asked by those preparing for the jaunt to Japan, "How long can this English-mania last? Surely someday another language will supplant "King Eigo" or the Japanese will just lose interest. And what about the many native speakers already going to Japan? Won't they toughen the competition?"

In response, I always encourage the inquirer to look to the Japanese culture for the answer. Since earliest times, the Japanese have followed the current leader. They are a generally humble folk who have a very realistic view of their place in the world: a small island nation full of industrious people.

As such, they know that they are destined to ride on bigger coattails than their own. Hundreds of years ago, those coattails belonged to China, from whom they imported their entire writing system. The biggest coattails to be seen today, however, are America's, a gargantuan country that won't soon be losing its "de facto" dominance.

The sheer size of the American population, nation and economy make the US the logical focus of Japan's energies. Just as the "daimyo" or feudal lords usually sought to increase their wealth by getting close to the "shogun" or warlord, so Japan seeks to be ever closer to America and the whole English-speaking world. For it is the 700,000,000 inhabitants of that world who control the vast majority of the planet's wealth and it is that wealth that Japan would like a part of and knows its well-being depends on.

The concern about an oversupply of English teachers is perhaps a more valid one. True, more native speakers are going to Japan to try their hand as "sensei" but the numbers are still miniscule. Because teachers are issued visas in the "catch-all" 4-1-16-3 category, even the government isn't quite sure how many there are in the country. Immigration's best estimate is only around 6,000 currently to which must be added a large number of "gaijin" teaching on either a cultural ("student") visa, special work-related visa or illegally as tourists.

Contrast that number (perhaps 10,000 foreigners) with an estimate made by *The Wall Street Journal* that as many as 10,000,000 adult Japanese may be currently enrolled in or looking for English conversation classes, most of which are taught by foreign instructors. I believe it's very safe to say that there are at least 1,000 Japanese looking for your services as a "sensei," a number which, even if cut in half, would still be more work than you could accept. Don't worry, the work *is* available and, given the high turnover rate among teachers and the growing interest in English, you're liable to be *more* in demand in the coming years, not less.

But what *is* the English teacher to the Japanese? Most involved in the industry would have to admit that actually teaching English is only a part of what a good teacher does in the classroom. The "affective" (emotional) components of the job are every bit as critical for successful instruction as getting the right response in drill.

You'll find that the vast majority of Japanese students of our language are terribly intent on learning it and work very hard at its study. More than a few of the adults you'll teach will be somewhat disheartened at having worked so hard for so many years only to find themselves unable to carry on a meaningful conversation with you. But actually learning to speak a foreign language (especially when the student's earlier focus has been on writing and reading) takes patience and practice.

For this reason, a big part of teaching will involve motivating and encouraging, whether the object of your attention is a ten-year-old who can't quite believe the noise you make is really a language or a grey-topped company president trying to share tidbits of corporate trivia with you. They'll all want to *talk* to you and it'll be up to you to help them do so naturally.

And that's where this teaching supplement to <u>JOBS IN JAPAN</u> comes in. I want to go into more detail with you now than space would permit in the earlier book and to explain just how I think a good, caring teacher can best help his or her Japanese students. I want to give you the tools you need and the confidence to use them, even if you've only been on the receiving end of a lectern in the past.

Your Japanese students, it should be remembered, may not be the most demonstrative people in their support of your efforts but, almost without exception, they really want you to succeed with them. For it is only by your success that they will have the whole world of opportunity that English represents open for them.

Helping anyone attain such a sought-after goal is a very large responsibility and it's my hope that by telling you something about our language and how best to practice our profession, you'll bring the kind of enthusiasm and concern to the classroom that the finest teachers seem to be able to summon up at will. With professional pride and care, you too can give the gift of our language to your students. And won't *that* kind of meaning in your work give you a thrill?!

The Development of Language

Consider if you will the humble bumble (bee, that is). Industrious, gregarious, gracious enough to share with us his wonderfully tasty regurgitations of the day's pollen-gathering--yes, man has much to admire about this prickly paradigm of our own society. But there's one quality about the bee that may make him our very closest kinsman in all the animal realm. Amazingly enough, the bee and man are the only two creatures on the planet that we know to be capable of non-contiguous communication. In other words, only we two beasties can tell our species of things happening outside the immediate area of communication.

Now, there may be those who resent having Shakespeare's sonnets compared to the animated wiggling of a drone trying to tell his hive of an especially appealing poinsetta but there is no other animal we know of that can convey information to its own kind about things outside where the "conversation" takes place. Lions roar, whales sing, dogs bark and they all qualify as a kind of language...but, as far as we know, only barely.

For the record, a language is simply "a system of arbitrary symbols by means of which a social group cooperates," at least according to linguist Bernard Bloch. In fact, language seems ready-made for man. Once our species decided to stand upright, we were relieved of having to hold our breath while using our arms for locomotion. On two legs, our relatively highly-placed vocal apparatus (tongue, vocal cords, jaw, teeth) is very well-suited to throwing a great number of distinct noises quite far.

Oddly enough, the primates, although blessed with more-or-less the same apparatus as ours, have no more instinctive language than any other animal. Only the parrot, with its keen ear for imitation, can even *sound* like it's communicating although it's totally incapable of original language.

Tightening the vocal cords causes a rise in pitch, which the Chinese and Scandanavians (among others) use to give the same word different meanings. Not allowing the vocal cords to vibrate is whispering, common to all languages. By positioning the tongue, teeth and uvula in the back of the throat, humans can make an astonishing number of distinct and regularly reproduceable sounds, almost all of which have meaning in some language somewhere.

But perhaps the most amazing feature of language is its infinite variety. The vast majority of utterances we encounter have never been heard by us before and yet we understand them, usually perfectly. There is no area of experience that is uncommunicable (as long as the conversants are willing to invest the time to explain) and there is no idea that can't be conveyed by those intent on its communication.

If you've been feeling somewhat intimidated by the speed and agility of today's computers, just ask an engineer about voice-recognition in his machine and how it compares to our own ability to understand almost any other speaker of our language talking about almost any subject. If he's honest, he'll tell you that even today's multi-million dollar silicon speedsters can't comprehend one-tenth the variety of voices and ideas the human mind can. (And, from what I understand, only the most sophisticated can dance around to tell other computers where especially delicious voltage can be found!)

Writing of all kinds apparently developed from picture signs: literal depictions of objects and actions. The Chinese and Japanese still use these "pictographs" (the Chinese use them exclusively, the Japanese in conjunction with two home-grown alphabets) but other cultures have developed more abstract forms to relieve the pictographs' tremendous strain on human memory.

The Greeks invented the first true alphabet by using consonantal characters in Phoenician script for which no sounds existed in Greek to represent vowels in their own language. From this Greek alphabet came the Cyrillic alphabet (used in Slavic languages, including Russian) and our own Roman alphabet.

Of course, as languages developed in small pockets of civilization, variations also developed. Dialects formed within linguistic populations too large to maintain a single form of speech, often as the result of influences from other languages. Still, speakers of these dialects could easily understand each other except when the number of dialects grew extreme.

Such a situation existed in Europe before the advent of telecommunications. Such a great number of dialects developed on the Continent that, for example, residents near the French-Roman frontier were at one time unintelligible by the residents of their respective capitals. The dialects could be understood by others immediately contiguous to the area and those contiguous dialects were understood by *their* neighbors but distant dialects may as well have been entirely different languages.

When distant trading became common, natives and foreign merchants alike needed to develop some common form of communication between their two alien societies. The "pidgin" languages that used bits and pieces of both languages (and sometimes a common third language as well) were purely economic tools that allowed the native producer and the foreign trader to dicker effectively on matters of business.

If trade were substantial enough and a particular pidgin became common enough to be passed on to later generations as their *first* language, the pidgin became a "creole". Haitian Creole, for example, shows lexical and grammatical structures from French and several African languages.

Much to the frustration of language teachers, no one is quite certain how even the dimmest member of a culture is able to learn his mother language as it is spoken in his immediate environment. But somehow, it's a gift every member of a society (regardless of genetic makeup) is given.

First-language acquisition occurs at a rapid pace and without apparent effort by a process called "grammar construction"--basically just trial and error usage of words and phrases heard around them. At the end of their first year, babies enlarge upon their repertoire of dozens of consistent (and highly effective!) preverbal communications and start making attempts to imitate words they hear around them. They will probably send their parents into fits of ecstasy at this stage by uttering their first "word", often just a misinterpreted belch.

By 18 months, the infant language student is stringing words together in two and three-word "sentences"--usually called "telegraphic" utterances due to their simple and effective content. By age three, he can chatter incessantly. (Long gone is the parents' delight at hearing him speak!)

By the time English-speaking children reach four, they can easily form plurals, the present progressive, past tense, third-person singular and possessives. (One study by Jean Berko found that a child of that age would conjugate the false word "gling" into "glinged" and sometimes "glang," suggesting a very sophisticated understanding of past tense formation.)

Behaviorists like B.F. Skinner believe that we learn by "operant conditioning", that is, the child "operates" language to get what it desires. And if "want milk" makes Mom bring the good stuff, the lesson is learned. The biggest problem with this theory, however, is the simple fact that most of what we say is perfectly novel and therefore unproven in operational effectiveness.

The great linguist, Noam Chomsky, was among those who suggested that we have within us the innate capacity to learn language, that we are biologically programmed to learn a language by a "Language Acquisition Device" or LAD. This LAD allows us to distinguish speech sounds from other environmental noise and construct the simplest possible system of language out of the language around us.

Whatever it is that allows us to so easily and readily learn our first language sadly disappears more or less at puberty. Although the difficulty of second-language learning has traditionally been blamed on "interference" with the first language, in fact, multi-linguals ("polyglots") really *can* learn several languages equally well and easily if they do so at a young age.

What seems more important in explaining the vastly increased difficulty we experience in learning a language in adulthood is what is generally called "lateralization" of the brain. This ongoing phenomenon is essentially an unconscious assigning of tasks by the individual to one side of the brain or the other.

As the child matures, the left hemisphere usually becomes increasingly dominant, emphasizing the analytical and intellectual aspects of the mind. Some think that once this dominance of the intellectual over the emotional side occurs, we tend to overanalyze and not be "free" enough in our efforts to learn a second language. Unlike children, it's possible that adult second language learners have become too rigid to just "go with the flow" in order to learn as easily as their infantile counterparts.

The Evolution of English

Luckily for us, we were able to master English before our LADs went bad. Because ours is such an exceptionally difficult language to learn with its many diverse linguistic influences, some foreigners actually believe that we native-speakers are a race of geniuses for being able to speak their target of intense study with such facility. Most students of our language, however, know that our command of the language was just plain dumb luck. The luck of having been born the descendants of nomads chasing woolly mammoths around the plains of southeast Europe about 5,000 years ago.

It was these nomads who spoke the granddaddy of English: Proto-Indo-European. From this proto-English, came (among such other exotics as Hindi and Sanskrit) three Germanic forms: East (now extinct), North (which evolved into the Scandanavian languages) and West (which became German, Dutch and, much later, English).

A major reason for the complexity of English is that it has been shaped by numerous invaders of the British Isles, each interweaving their own language into the existing amalgam. Among the earliest such conquerors were the Romans who occupied much of the islands, adding Latin in pre-Christian days to the native Celtic. Then, in the fifth and sixth centuries, Saxons, Jutes and Frisians crossed to England from Denmark and northern Germany. Along with them came the tribe that would come to name the country and our language: the Angles, named after an "angle" or corner of land between Schleswig and Flensburg near the German-Danish border.

After depositing such delightful peculiarities into the language as the mutated plurals *feet, geese, teeth, men, women, lice* and *mice*, the Germanic tribes were conquered by the Vikings who left us many down-to-earth words including *nay* for *no* and *fro* for *from.* The modern language closest to the Old English of that time is to be found in Iceland today.

In the 12th and 13th centuries, after the French invasion, there was actually a chance that English would die out all together as the French conquerors dominated British politics, science and the arts. Fortunately (perhaps *un*fortunately in the eyes of some students of the language), events sustained English.

In 1362, Parliament began officially using English instead of French and during that same period, the prime literary spokesman of the era, Geoffrey Chaucer, chose to write in English, despite his fluency in French. Today, as a result of France's most recent foreign rule of England, most of the words of learning, refinement and power are French-based, while earlier Scandanavian and Germanic words are used for more common purposes. The half-million general words in the English vocabulary are about evenly divided between the two sources.

English today is certainly one of the most flexible and adaptable languages in the world, largely due to its relatively few inflections (form changes), which, in other languages, tend to "lock" forms and not allow variations within a grammar. German, for example, is highly inflected with five forms for the word *man.* Chinese, at the opposite extreme, has only one form. English has four but, unlike other European languages, only inflects nouns, pronouns and verbs, not adjectives (except *this, that, these* and *those*). For example, only in English do we use *tall* to describe both men and women. Other European languages all use inflected forms, such as the Spanish *alta* or *alto*, depending on the gender of the object described.

This lack of inflections and, hence, rigidity has allowed English-speakers to be delightfully imaginative in creating new forms. Now we can "plan a table" or "table a plan", "lift a thumb" or "thumb a lift." In all other languages in our "family", nouns and verbs can never be interchangeable due to their special grammatical endings.

The real richness in development of the language today, however, lies in the use of affixes. Added either to the front ("prefix"), back ("suffix") or middle ("infix"), these are the building blocks of modern English. The word suffix "-er," for example, can denote the doer of an action (*farmer*), the instrument (*harvester*), or the area (*New Yorker*).

"Composition" lets us join words to create altogether new compound words. *Already* has come to differ from *all ready*. A *gentle man* may or not be a *gentleman*. (The Chinese use composition very freely to create words like *fly machine* for *airplane*, and *lightening language* for *telephone*.)

"Back-formations" are intriguing words, created by the mistaken extension of words back to non-existent stems. For example, *to edit* was derived from *editor* by some long-forgotten goof who wrongly assumed that the words are related to each other in the way *actor* is to act. Likewise, to bulldoze, to televise, and to commute are also new words with no true etymology.

"Blends" are also very popular and becoming more so, especially in politics and in pop culture. Bang and smash become *bash*; smoke and fog become *smog*, while a motor cavalcade becomes a *motorcade* and a cable telegram becomes a *cablegram*. (The Japanese are famous for their fondness for blends. "Radio-cassette" is apparently too cumbersome to say so it is routinely shortened to "*raji-kase*." while "telephone communications" sometimes becomes "*tere-komi*.")

Thanks to world trade, we now have commonplace words in our vocabularies from all over the world. *Sugar* is Arabic, *chess* is Persian, *cherub* is Hebrew, *mammoth* is Russian, *robot* is Czech, *bizarre* is Basque, *shampoo* is Hindi, *ketchup* is Malay, *hurricane* is from the Caribbean and *kangaroo* (you might have guessed this one) is Aboriginal Australian.

The Latin alphabet had all the letters of our modern Roman alphabet except j, k, v, w, y and z. The Romans added k to help with abbreviations and y and z to help transcribe Greek. W was added (as you might guess) as a double u while j and v were added as consonant variants of i and u. Today, we use all 26 letters in both uppercase, or capital, and lowercase, or small, letters.

These 26 letters are used to represent the 44 sounds of English with its 12 vowels, 9 diphthongs (vowel combinations) and 23 consonants. These consonants include six "plosives" (p, b, t, d, k, and g), six "fricatives" (f, v, th as in *thin*, th as in *then*, s, z, sh as in *ship*, s as in *pleasure*, and h), two "affricatives (ch as in *church* and j), the nasals (m, n and ng as in *young*), the "lateral" l, the "retroflex" r, and the "semivowels" y and w. Three of the letters (q, c, and x) are redundant since they duplicate either k or ks.

Unlike the sounds of the consonants which are the same wherever English is spoken, the language's five vowels are pronounced differently according to dialect. American English has 13 vowel sounds and four diphthongs (blended vowels). The American vowels include those sounds found in *eat, sit, ate, get, had, not, saw, so, put, you, son, her,* and *up*. The diphthongs are the vowel sounds in *I, cow, boy,* and *few*. Again, these sounds are only for the North American dialect and will vary widely in other countries and sometimes in North America itself, depending on what is standard pronunciation in the region.

Critics of the language claim that we have too few letters representing too many sounds--it's bound to make spelling confusing. On the other hand, our consonants and consonant clusters are fairly unambiguous, we don't use diacritical marks above the letters like French, German, Spanish, Russian and other European languages and just about anyone familiar with any Latin or any Romance language can make a pretty good guess as to the meaning of an unfamiliar word. (Unfortunately, this doesn't do the Japanese student a lot of good.)

At least as difficult as spelling for the Japanese student is the fact that English is a heavily stressed language which uses stress and emphasis in very meaningful ways. For example, *record* and *permit*, are changed from nouns to verbs just by shifting the stress from the first to second syllable. Consider, too, the different nuances possible by changing emphasis from one word to the next in the sentence, *I walked to the theater*. By emphasizing different words, different questions can be answered with that one sentence: *Who walked to the theater? How did you get to the theater?* and *Where did you walk to?* (Most grammarians now accept the placement of prepositions at the end of sentences as standard.)

Over time, an American dialect developed which was codified and formalized thanks largely to the efforts of Samuel Webster who, by writing his <u>American Dictionary of the English Language</u> in 1828, set down once and for all what it was that those upstart provincials were saying.

The dictionary set the American practice of writing -er for -re (e.g., *theater*), -or for -our (*favor*), *check* for *cheque*, *connection* for *connexion*, *jail* for *gaol*, and a few others. Aside from these and the obvious lexical differences between the dialects (e.g., *elevator* for *lift*), Americans, unlike the British, don't usually consider collective nouns as plurals (the audience were), but do actively change nouns to verbs (to author). Americans generally use *will* rather than *shall* and *have got* for *have*. Americans also customarily pronounce the unstressed syllables that Britons often drop, such as *lab'ratory* instead of the British *laborat'ry*.

Differences between "British Received Pronunciation" and "General American" today are really quite few and dwindling fast thanks to global communications. The British still pronounce the vowels in *box* and *caught* similarly, and *bath* and *bother* similarly. They also tend to lose the r sound following vowels (as in *door*).

Today, largely because of the immense size and influence of America and its impact on world events, American English is the standard in those parts of the world outside Britain's immediate sphere of influence (e.g., Europe). In Japan, "the King's English" was preferred for decades until Japan's trade with America skyrocketed and Britain's influence on the world stage faded somewhat.

But like any dialect anywhere, neither British nor American English is considered any "better" than the other. There is no such thing as "bad" English so long as members of the speaker's group share that speech pattern and don't view it as non-standard.

Popular Teaching Methodologies

Once man decided to interact with his foreign fellows, second language learning became essential. The first "world language" (at least in the Western world) was Greek, language of the dominant culture and a convenient medium of communication for the trading nations of the Mediterranean. Formalized learning of other languages, however, began with the Romans around the third century B.C. when they realized that the Greek civilization had much to teach them.

This study of Greek encouraged the Romans to define the workings of their own Latin and by the first century B.C., Latin was being taught regularly throughout the empire, becoming the second world language and serving that function well into the 18th Century as learned men and women of the West used it in their business, culture and religion.

The usual method of learning Latin and indeed other languages up to the last century was "grammar translation." This excruciatingly boring process had the students study long lists of grammatical rules and vocabulary of the target language, then spend hours translating passages back and forth from one language to the other.

Very little time was spent in using the language for free communication of student thoughts, a limitation which virtually guaranteed that the student would have tremendous difficulty ever using the target language for anything but more tedious translation. Sadly, "grammar translation" is the method of choice of Japanese public schools for the learning of English, encouraging private schools to go to the opposite extreme of almost never stressing instruction in English grammar in their classes. Other methods are considerably more humane.

The "natural method" developed in Europe in response to the ineffectiveness of grammar-translation. Naturalists believed it should be possible for a student to learn a second language as he had learned his first: by exposure and figuring things out in his own unique way.

They argued that 1) repetition is as important for second language learners as for first; 2) language learning is mostly an imitative act; 3) the sequence of learning must be sounds, then words, then whole sentences; 4) listening, then speaking should be taught; 5) reading and writing are more advanced skills than speaking and listening; 6) translation shouldn't be necessary and 7) grammar instruction should not be called for since, after all, children are rarely taught or even aware of their mother tongue's grammar.

Unfortunately, users of this method found that the student's first language interfered with learning the second and that the natural method didn't take advantage of the mature student's ability to logically analyze the second language to facilitate learning. Nor was there the same motivation in the second language as existed in the first. The child is essentially mute until he learns his first language. The second language student can already get by quite nicely in his mother tongue and so doesn't have quite the same sense of urgency no matter how driven he may be to speak the target language.

The "direct method" is probably the most popular method in language instruction today. With it, the student's own language is never used, creating a different world in the classroom in which the target language is the only acceptable mode of communication. As used by the Berlitz schools (probably the method's biggest booster), the teacher presents a story and students memorize entire sentences from it, later answering questions about the story. Grammar and vocabulary are taught incidentally or at the end of the lesson.

One of the best variations on the direct method is that used by the US military which emphasizes teaching of the target language's culture as well as the language itself. Classes are very intensive, taught only by a native speaker who emphasizes colloquial rather than formal speech. The success rate of students is quite high but not many ordinary classes could allow 15 hour per week sessions and regular extracurricular sessions with native speakers.

In reaction to earlier emphasis on reading, a type of direct method called the "audiolingual method" (or ALM) became quite popular in the 1960's and '70's. With this "aural-oral" method, material is first presented in a dialog in a highly controlled way to minimize student errors. The students then mimic and memorize ("mim-mem") some of what the teacher has read. Later, drills are used to manipulate the various grammatical structures introduced although little formal analysis of grammar is done. Outside of class, there is regular use of language laboratories where students mimic native speakers' tapes, emphasizing pronunciation.

ALM counted on repetition of material to form habits of speech which would cause learners to use the target language automatically. This was believed to be a much more "natural" approach and one that allowed the second language learner to approximate the same path taken by him when he learned his first language.

Some linguists like the renowned Noam Chomsky, however, believed that adult learners needed to have their intellects engaged for effective language learning. He and his followers offered the "cognitive" approach as an alternative and the battle between "rote" and "meaningful" learning was begun.

In the mid-1960s, the cognitive approach emphasized use of the target language for free communication and freely explained grammar rules to that end. Pronunciation was deemphasized with the reasoning that it was pointless if not impossible to sound like a native speaker. Errors were seen as signs of development and inevitable. Silence was seen as a useful part of internalization of the language and repetition (if not personally meaningful) was considered of limited value.

In 1972, Caleb Gattegno introduced one of the most innovative methods called "The Silent Way." With it, the teacher is largely a facilitator and speaks as little as possible, trying constantly to engage the student's mind.

Props are frequently used by the teacher using this method, usually a set of small colored rods which she places in different configurations for the student's analysis, modeling the correct utterance only once.

Because students are frequently left to figure such configurations out on their own without a lot of teacher assistance, there is indeed a great deal of silence in the lesson. Proponents of the method, however, believe that, as with other cognitive methods, this is useful silence in which the student's mind is working, or as Gattegno puts it, "throwing the learner on himself." Supposedly, lessons learned this way are more meaningful and consequently more memorable, but some teachers find the lack of repetition and assistance and the rigid presentation of new material somewhat stifling.

One interesting and much-discussed new method is "counseling learning," developed by Charles Curran and later adopted in linguistics as Community Language Learning (CLL). In this, the class of language students is assembled in a circle with a native speaker facilitator (or "knower") wandering behind them. Anytime one student wishes to talk to another about anything at all, he may do so by addressing the group in the target language. If he can't say what he wants to, he speaks in his native language and the facilitator makes a translation which the student then repeats to the individual addressed.

At the end of a fifteen minute session, a tape recording of it is analyzed by the group. In its final stages, color-coded lights are used to signal non-verbally to the group if an error has been made, if a more suitable expression could be used or if the communication was correct. Unfortunately, time constraints and the scarcity of truly bilingual facilitators make CLL something of a luxury.

Asher's Total Physical Response found great popularity in the late 1970's as it encouraged students to get physically involved in the target language. The teacher restricted his instructions to the target language and told students to move about the classroom, performing various common tasks such as opening the door, erasing the blackboard, giving paper to another student, etc. It was believed (and still is by many) that such movement reinforces the language lesson.

The results with TPR have been impressive. Within thirty minutes of first-time instruction, students of Japanese have been able to correctly respond to the teacher's instruction: "Isu kara tatte, kokuban ni anata no namae o kese." ("Stand up and write your name on the blackboard.") And best of all, retention even after one year was excellent.

"Suggestology" (or "suggestopedia") is a faintly mystical method developed in Eastern Europe by Bulgarian psychologist Georgi Lozanov. Lozanov maintains that his method is appropriate not only for language learning but for any subject. Basically, it seeks to overcome negative "suggestions" or inhibitions which block learning. Such fears include feelings of incompetence, fear of making mistakes and apprehension toward the unfamiliar.

To accomplish this, suggestology makes liberal use of mood creation. Music is frequently played to relax students and the teacher assumes the role of almost a therapist, exceedingly trustworthy and gentle. Classrooms ideally resemble living rooms wherein the student's comfort is of paramount importance so as to open the avenues of learning.

Students are given new names in the target culture and encouraged to assume a new identity in the classroom. Homework is minimal but students are asked to come to class somewhat familiar with the many dialogs presented each lesson. These dialogs are initially read by the teacher with background mood music and finally in concert by the students. Conversation is encouraged with extensive correction coming only much later in the course.

Critics say suggestology students lack accurate grammar but there's no denying that they are generally more fluent by virtue of their lessened inhibitions. Because they are usually more willing to communicate, they have been shown to acquire proficiency at a faster rate than students taught by more traditional methods.

Such affective (dare we call them "touchy-feely?") methods as suggestology come from a growing concern in linguistic circles for personality variables in second language learning. Alexander Guiora suggests that there is such a thing as a "language ego" which, in essence, is the persona the student adopts in the language classroom. Guiora says that ego and self-identity are inseparable parts of learning a language because communication is such a fundamentally human activity.

He makes a good point in stating that children learn their first language at a time when their egos are growing and flexible. The new language poses no "threat" to their self-esteem so the child can freely practice the language (and more importantly, make mistakes) without feeling stupid or inept. Puberty apparently defines the ego and establishes defense mechanisms which discourage the adult language learner from taking chances and "acting like a fool" to practice the language.

Along these same lines, Guiora conducted a test among students of Thai. By administering small amounts of alcohol, he found that a student's pronunciation improves markedly once inhibitions are somewhat lessened, even by artificial means. But, although it appears that students really would speak better with a pre-class cocktail, there hasn't been any evidence that other aspects of language except pronunciation improve with booze. Still, in my view, inhibition and fear of errors are primary causes of the dismal record Japanese students have with English.

This wealth of methods alternately emphasizing or prohibiting the mother tongue, grammar study and even errors in the classroom demonstrates just how imprecise the art of language instruction is. Even academics who have built their tenure on the study of the effectiveness of such methodologies will occasionally confess to not knowing what works best. Everyone does agree, however that the student's sincere desire to learn and the teacher's enthusiasm are probably key.

Students usually don't enjoy saying what is incomprehensible to them but they do enjoy sharing a true thought in a foreign language. They loathe what they see as meaningless tasks and dislike mechanical repetitions. Most of all, language students don't learn unless they *want* to. Motivation and personal involvement are the bedrock upon which success in a foreign language rests.

Teaching English as a Foreign Language

The field of endeavor you are about to enter is alternately known as TEFL, TESL, TEAL, TESP, TESOL or TENES depending on the type of English you teach and your desire to confuse or be confused by the person to whom you are describing your work. Although some people tend to use the terms interchangeably, TEFL correctly refers only to Teaching English as a Foreign Language, that is, in an environment such as Japan where English is not a standard medium of communication.

TESL means Teaching English as a Second Language and it describes teaching English to someone such as an immigrant to America who will be using the language on a regular basis for everyday life. It also describes the teaching of English in places like the Philippines where native languages like Tagalog are primary but English is a nationally-known second language.

TEAL is an intelligent (and clever) way to deal with the fact that English may represent neither a foreign nor a second language to the learner. (Many English students, in fact, are quite fluent in several languages.) Teaching English as Another Language is probably the most neutral description of the pedagogy and it's a term the Canadian teaching community is especially fond of. Not only is the Canadian association of such teachers called TEAL but their emblem nicely combines the definitions of the word the acronym forms. Still, we can't help but wonder if a blue duck on one's letterhead lends the proper air of decorum to correspondence. Might the recipient not think he was being approached by the local wildlife commission? Oh well, especially in teaching, chuckles are always appreciated.

TESP is an up-and-coming area of instruction wherein instructors teach English for Special Purposes. This practice has developed to meet the needs of people like engineers who don't really have the time to learn "this is a pen" but have a great yearning to learn such utterances as "this is a variable transducer." Schools offering ESP courses all over the world are in great need of professional people with specialized knowledge willing and able to teach their jargon to eager English students.

TESOL is best known as the name of the largest professional organization for ESL/EFL teachers. But it also stands simply for Teachers of English to Speakers of Other Languages, a nice catchall description which rivals only TENES or Teachers of English to Non-English Speakers for top honors in blandness. The rule of thumb for the field is, if you're teaching overseas, it's probably TEFL and if you're teaching domestically, it's probably TESL.

Unfortunately, despite the huge demand for EFL instructors worldwide, there has been little agreement as to what methods or tools work best. The primary reason for this (aside from the relative youth of the field) is that every student is as different as every teacher and no one knows what combination, with materials used as catalyst, is most effective.

Generally speaking, lessons are "sequenced" from easy to difficult. There are certain fundamental elements of the language (such as the "be" verb) which must be firmly in place before the student can progress to more sophisticated forms. The "Quick Guide to English Grammar" in the Appendix is sequenced in a more-or-less appropriate manner for students.

More and more, however, ESL/EFL teachers are moving away from the traditional grammar sequencing syllabus and toward what's called the "notional-functional syllabus." This means that while there remains sequencing of grammatical forms based on degree of difficulty, the teacher doesn't just teach, for example, everything the student has never wanted to know about gerunds. Instead, he will teach in a typical lesson everything the student might need to know, for example, to order in a restaurant.

Frequently, the lesson will loosely revolve around a particular grammar point appropriate to the "function" being presented (for example, use of "I'll have"), but mostly it's an effort to teach students discrete chunks of survival-type English, immediately usable in their daily lives. As you'd imagine, this is especially popular and useful for people living in the country of the target language.

In EFL, it is typical to introduce a lesson and grammatical structure with a dialog, usually between two speakers. Ideally, the dialog should include material recently learned by the students as well as one or two new items which will serve as a focus of the lesson. Speakers' lines should be short but very natural. Greetings for the speakers aren't necessary unless they are part of the lesson; they usually tend to slow down the readings.

Some teachers have their students memorize the dialog. Many Japanese students refuse to do this or any other rote memorization, however, if they're just taking the class for fun. Far better for such students are choral, group and finally individual readings of the dialog as well as personal explanation of the lesson's target structure.

In keeping with today's "cognitive" approach to language learning, use of the student's native language isn't usually forbidden but it certainly is discouraged. Still, if the teacher knows the students' language, a lot of time can be saved by presenting a brief explanation in that language rather than having to resort to convoluted and confusing elaborations in the target language.

Probably the single most important thing the language teacher can bear in mind as she stands in front of her class is that it is not her show. The tremendous amount of "teacher talk" produced by instructors who feel obliged to "perform" for the students and keep up non-stop patter lest the students start snoozing has been a problem since the Romans told their students how to learn Greek rather than letting them practice it themselves. The good teacher speaks in class only enough to get the students talking in the target language.

One good way to encourage students to take a more active part in the class is to assign small classroom-management tasks to them. Students can call roll, return corrected papers, read announcements, etc. These chores, however minor, can develop a sense of teamwork, the learning of names and, most importantly, that it's the students' class too and they should take an active role in it.

Teachers are fairly evenly divided as to the desirability of assigning names in the target language to students. I prefer to let students select English names from my pre-approved list (see Appendix) because the foreign name not only gives them good pronunciation practice but it also allows the student to assume a "safe" role in the classroom. As "Larry," he can afford to make mistakes but as the real "Tanaka-san," he might feel inhibited by his position in his company or by the presence of his class/workmates. When assigning names, try to make them ones which will "stretch" the students' pronunciation.

Teachers also must decide whether to use an inductive or deductive approach in presenting new material. If you prefer to teach inductively, you just present material without explanation and expect your students to discern in their own way what was happening language-wise in the reading, drill, or whatever. A deductive approach, of course, is just the opposite with rules explained first, then examples given to demonstrate those rules in action.

Many teachers combine the two by administering a dialog first without explanation of the new structure presented and giving a few examples of what's happening linguistically. This allows the students the opportunity to form some idiosyncratic rules about it, then explain the rule at work as they think it can best be stated. Drill and examples drawn from students' personal experiences then help to reinforce knowledge of it. All in all, though, the deductive approach is favored, simply because both teachers and students generally prefer to know what's going on at the outset of the lesson.

The usual steps taken in the teaching of a particular lesson are:

* Determining what students need to be taught.
* Finding or creating a realistic dialog or other reading demonstrating this point.
* Modeling it to the students.
* Having the group, then individuals, read it.
* Explaining what is being taught by it by stating the language rules at work.
* Checking for understanding by suggesting different situations where the structure might be used.
* Practicing the structure with drills so it becomes internalized.
* Expanding it into personal and independent communication by having the students describe their own experiences using the new structure.
* Reviewing the structure at a later time to reinforce it and ensure retention.

Corrections of students should be handled delicately. It's generally acknowledged now that mistakes are a natural and probably necessary part of learning a language. It's important not to make the student feel foolish for making them. At the same time, it's equally important not to let the student think his major flub was acceptable English. Many teachers favor "expansions" for this purpose so the student isn't made to feel like a dolt but also gets the message that he misspoke.

Essentially, when the teacher expands on what the student says, he "echoes" back what was said but in the correct form. The student might say, for example, "I told my friend I going to America" and the teacher would reply with something like "Yes, I remember when I told my friend I was going to Japan."

Denser students might very well think your expansions are just inane comments, of course, so it's probably a good idea to inform the class of how this corrective practice works so they listen attentively to what you're echoing back to them. For those who still don't get it, you can get the student to correct himself by leading him back to where his language failed by saying, in this case, "I told my friend I...?"

Many times, a student will consistently fail to correct a grammatical error despite repeated corrections by the teacher. One reason for this may be that the error has become "fossilized" or fixed in the student's mind, probably because some earlier teacher failed to correct it. Such bad linguistic habits are tough to break but making the student aware that he is unconsciously making the same mistake regularly usually causes him to pay attention to it.

Another type of common error is what results from a learner's "interlanguage." The interlanguage, linguists believe, is an idiosyncratic way of speaking which almost all language learners develop to allow them simple communication. It's not a major problem as long as it is merely a temporary stage in their acquisition of the language. But if, for example, the student consistently drops the final -s in third person singular constructions ("he *work* in Osaka") for too long without correction, such errors can become "fossilized." The world is full of people who speak a foreign language very comfortably and confidently--and very badly.

It's very important not to interrupt a good flow of target language use with corrections. If the teacher is part of a give-and-take conversation with a student, expansions can correct usage in a fairly unobtrusive way. Students frequently will ask teachers to correct them whenever they make a mistake but it quickly becomes obvious that conversation would be virtually impossible with constant corrections.

A better way to keep the flow going and correct students is to keep a log of individual students' mistakes. Most students have particular areas of grammar in which they are shaky and subtle notes during student speeches, drills and group exercises can quickly identify them for later work.

A student's area of weakness can also be spotted by regular "avoidance" of a particular structure. You may find that a particular student will bend over backwards to avoid using the present perfect ("I have seen"), preferring to always use, say, the simple past tense ("saw") which many times works perfectly well. Avoidance can be recognized many times by the student opting for a more complex or longer sentence rather than one using a simple, but difficult sound or grammatical construction.

Vocabulary, of course, is an essential element of language instruction but there can be too much of a good thing. Japanese students tend to have impressive vocabularies thanks to their public school's emphasis on grammar-translation. Unfortunately, like a computer without a program, there's not much they can do with all those words until they learn how to make them work together.

Teachers generally agree nowadays that it's a poor idea to teach vocabulary items in isolation. The words need to be associated with something meaningful in the student's life, if only that lesson's dialog. The first words you'll want to teach (if the students have forgotten them), of course, are the ones necessary for the class: listen, repeat, say, ask, and answer.

It should also be explained to students early on that there are content-type words (with meaning) and there are function-type words (for grammar, e.g. the). The Japanese are especially keen to learn the derivatives of lexical (dictionary) meanings. Teaching travel, traveler and well-traveled shows the student how English affixes work and makes vocabulary-building seem logical. Be careful, however, not to teach so many derivatives that the students become overwhelmed. Three of four derivates per item is probably best.

An intermediate EFL student should probably have a vocabulary of about 2,000 English words. These should include all numbers (both cardinal and ordinal), dates, addresses, measurements (such as age, weight, height, time, distance and money), common foods, days of the week, months, seasons, clothing, utensils, body parts, furniture, family relationships, colors, shapes and sizes, cities and countries, common animals, common occupations, common activities. Either written or orally, you might want to give a brief test on these items to your class to see who knows what. Many times, students will know incredibly sophisticated words but will have gaping holes in their knowledge of everyday terms.

Idioms and slang (the "spice" of any language) are always popular items of study and, since they are a very real part of our language, should certainly be shared with students. It's very important, however, to explain thoroughly to students at the time these are presented that they are not appropriate for all situations--usually only the most casual. If, thanks to your failure to warn him, the Japanese student someday asks his conservative American client if he wouldn't like to "toss back some brewskies" with him after work, you might have done him a bit of a disservice.

"Register" refers to the speaker's level of formality which may change according to the social environment. It isn't a social or regional dialect but rather a special variety of language used for a specific purpose. A primary way to distinguish a child's use of language from that of an adult is the degree to which she is able to vary styles according to the social situation.

Linguist Martin Joos in his fascinating book, The Five Clocks, refers to five different levels of formality in English, each with different forms of speech: the oratorical or frozen level, the deliberative or formal level, the consultative level, the casual level and the intimate level.

The oratorical style, says Joos, is used mostly in public speaking with carefully chosen wording, somewhat exaggerated intonation and many rhetorical devices. The deliberative style is used when size of the audience makes personal interaction impossible. It is a more informal style than the oratorical but words are also carefully chosen for essentially pure information transmission such as one might find in a large university lecture.

Businessmen and doctors use the consultative style with clients wherein words are still carefully chosen and formality is maintained. Casual style is used among friends where social barriers are few and words are not especially guarded. An intimate style is used among close friends and family members with whom complete honesty can be granted without inhibitions.

In Japan, especially, conversation is king. Students all clamor for it and school officials all promise it to them in the form of a real-live native speaker. Unfortunately, there's a terrific potential for a real waste of time if the teacher spends all of his time trying to get students to engage in free conversation before they're relaxed or prepared enough. Oftentimes, too, the teacher feels compelled to address "significant issues" during the conversation period when, in fact, students often prefer simple but sincere inquiries into their own lives, so long as the teacher isn't intrusive.

Free conversation certainly plays an essential role in language acquisition but too often, such sessions wind up with the teacher doing all the talking, having the "conversation" dominated by a handful of assertive students or (every teacher's worst nightmare) dead silence while the desperate teacher tries to get the students to say something, *anything!*

Make sure that you have sufficient rapport with the students and that they have the linguistic tools available before you throw open the doors of conversation. Many times, your students will need a lot of preliminary work before they engage in meaningful conversation.

Rather than opening the class to free conversation, often engaging the students in "role play" serves the same purpose but gives better focus to the proceedings. For example, if the day's lesson has been on the wh- question words (who, what, etc.), students could be paired off and told they are a newspaper reporter and a crime victim or a detective and his suspect. Since so many English students in Japan are businessmen, role plays about meeting a foreign businessperson are especially popular and useful, almost qualifying as ESP (English for Special Purposes).

Breaking the class up into small groups is an excellent way to multiply the amount of time each student speaks in class. In my view, small groups should be formed as much as possible and whenever the students can be given something substantive to work on for at least 10 minutes.

There are conflicting views in teaching about how to structure small groups. Some teachers like to cluster all the dominant students in a single group to allow the more reticent ones to speak freely whereas other teachers believe more articulate students act as catalysts for quieter students and so they should be mingled.

In a homogeneous class like those of Japan, the teacher must be very strict about not allowing Japanese to be spoken. The students probably will feel foolish speaking broken English to each other when their natural language is so accessible but they will comply if they know you're serious about it. Some teachers set up a "fine" system whereby students must contribute, for example, fifty yen to a "party kitty" each time they slip up and use Japanese.

Drills are an important part of every language class, much as students (and some teachers) may loathe them. They're still the most effective means we have to demonstrate how a grammatical structure functions and alters, to reinforce it in the mind of the student, and to test the student's comprehension of it.

The well-respected EFL/ESL academic, Wilga Rivers, suggests that teachers remember the following "rules of drill":

* Drills are for teaching not testing.
* Give plenty of practice in each element before moving to the next.
* Stick to one specific structural element (don't try to teach more than one thing per drill).
* The feature you're drilling should have been part of an earlier activity (e.g., a dialogue).
* Keep changes from one item to the next small.
* Keep the items short.
* Each item should be a natural, realistic utterance.
* The teacher's cue should ideally prompt only one proper response.
* Keep vocabulary simple.
* Drill orally and only in the target language.

* Vary the types of drill.
* Arrange for students to use drill material in meaningful communication immediately after the drill is completed.

The most common "manipulative" drills are repetition, substitution (either single- or multiple-slot), transformation, completion, expansion, paraphrasing and integrative. Among "meaningful" drills we have restatements and rejoinders, and question and answer.

<u>Repetition</u> is simply having students echo back exactly what the teacher says, usually first as a group (choral), then smaller groups (e.g., first males, then females; right side of class, then left side of class) and finally individuals, either volunteers or "victims."

<u>Single-slot substitution drills</u> have the students given a sentence or question and cue word. They must then insert the cue word in the same place in the sentence. For example: "I go to the store every day. Week." = "I go to the store every week."

<u>Multiple-slot substitution drills</u> simply allow the student to place the new word anywhere in the original sentence where it would be correct. For example: "I go to the park every week. He." = "He goes to the park every week." Then "movies" = "He goes to the movies every week."

<u>Transformation drills</u> have the student change the form of the sentence or question. For example, "I go to the store every week." = "Do you go to the store every week?" This works especially well in *chains* where one student will transform a structure and direct it to another student who then continues with another; e.g., "Now ask Tomoko." It's a good way to help minimize "teacher talk."

<u>Completion drills</u> can only be used with certain structural types, such as tag questions. The student merely adds to what the teacher says; e.g., "He went to the store today." = "He went to the store today, didn't he?"

<u>Expansion drills</u> are very common to help students digest complex sentences when they can't remember the whole thing in a single mental gulp. For example, if the teacher for some odd reason wants the students to say, "I thought I saw a purple cow but, after careful consideration, I decided I must have been mistaken," he

would probably have to "build" them to it by starting with, "I thought I saw" (they repeat), "I thought I saw a purple cow" (repeat), until they have retained the full utterance.

Paraphrasing drills can be tricky because they require the student to create a new form. But with sharp intermediate or advanced students who have thoroughly studied what is being drilled, they can be very effective. For example, if you've been explaining how verbs can be made into nouns by adding -ed, you might instruct them to paraphrase "the decorator put carpet on the floor." = "The decorator carpeted the floor."

In teaching affixes (both prefixes and suffixes), paraphrasing can elicit the desired structure. If, for example, you've been teaching un-, you might say, "if the door is locked and you want to get out, you would tell me to..." = "Unlock the door, please."

Integrative drills are very useful to get students to speak more efficiently since it encourages the compounding of phrases. For example, "I went to the store. He went to the store." = "I went to the store and he did too."

Meaningful drills are those which ask the student to give personal meaning to the response. Restatement drills have the student rephrase a question, often readdressing it in "chain" fashion to another student. For example: "Toshi, ask Hiromi what she did yesterday" = "Hiromi, what did you do yesterday." "I went to the library. Sadahiro, what did you do yesterday?" and so forth around the room.

Rejoinder drills require a fairly high level of proficiency but are excellent practice for real communication. They require the student to listen critically to what the teacher is saying and actually correct a misperception. For example, if the teacher says "Yasuo, what countries border Canada besides Japan and Mexico?" the student should say something like "Japan doesn't border Canada and neither does Mexico." A simple version of this has the student reply to the teacher with some personal information; e.g., "I don't smoke." = "You don't smoke and neither do I."

Many people don't regard question- and-answer as a drill at all, but it could be considered one if the student incorporates the target vocabulary into his response. "What's your hobby?" = "My hobby is playing golf." It would probably not be a true drill if the student had simply replied, "I like to play golf."

In drilling, it's important not to "telegraph" your selected "victim" before stating the problem. If students know they won't be called on, many of them won't bother trying to work the exercise. It's best to state the drill problem, wait a few seconds for *all* the students to think about it and reach an answer, then select a student to respond.

In selecting students, teachers need to be aware of favoritism, often caused by a reluctance to embarrass students whom they think might not know the answer. A study of this in 1977 showed that teachers indeed don't distribute turns evenly but instead rely on either the brighter students, those who for some reason "look ready" or worse, where the students are sitting in the classroom!

A more equitable system might be to put student names on index cards and just work your way through the stack. To effectively match bright or slow students with the challenging and easier questions, respectively, you could remove student names from the stack of cards after they had answered correctly and then choose from among the remaining students according to the question's difficulty. The problem with this, of course, is that the students who have already answered will know they won't be called on and might not do the drill. It's always best to keep 'em guessing!

Group work is especially good for managing a large class but should also be used liberally in any class since it reduces "teacher talk." Some Japanese students may think this is an unusual way to conduct a class since, in their minds, they came to work with a "gaijin," not listen to other Japanese speak broken English.

If you hear such a comment, a good response is that the class is for speaking, not hearing practice and is designed to improve their own personal fluency. It's largely irrelevant whether the hearer of the speaker's efforts is Japanese or native English speaker.

In Japan, your class may be the students' first experience with group work since probably all their other instruction used the lecture format. Therefore, it's probably a good idea to spend part of the first class period explaining the desirability of working in groups and how it will allow each student to spend more time speaking English as students act alternately as student and teacher. Students will also need assurance that the teacher will always be close at hand to answer questions and correct major mistakes as she circles throughout the classroom.

Students should be divided into groups of three to six, depending on the total class size so that you have probably no more than about eight groups. For large classes, a leader should be elected in each group, perhaps after the students have had a chance to evaluate each other's English proficiency by having everyone introduce himself in English.

The leader might then gather members' names, addresses and telephone numbers which are submitted to the teacher. It's always a good idea to have some means of contacting your students in case of emergency and tasking group leaders with calling their group's members saves a lot of phone time.

Speeches and debates are challenging and very useful for the Japanese student if only to help them overcome their extreme reluctance to speak publicly. Assigning prepared speeches allows the student sufficient time to feel confident about what he has written but impromptu speeches most closely approximate using English for communication. Subjects should be kept simple and innocuous at first, gradually becoming more controversial and complex as students improve their English and feel more at ease with each other.

Traditional debates have three students on a side giving the presentation, rebuttal and summation, respectively. Judges can be recruited from students unable to debate because of absences in their teams with the teacher reserving veto power in case of favoritism.

Teaching English in Japan

English instruction is a huge preoccupation among the Japanese people. Although English is not a required subject in high school, the fact that it is an important part of the dreaded college-entrance exams encourages students to take it the whole time they attend junior and high school. With close to 100% of Japanese graduating from high school, it's probably safe to say that over 90% of adult Japanese have studied the language for six or more years.

The 1/3 of high school graduates who continue on to college typically take the subject for an additional four years so the majority of people whom the average foreigner in Japan encounters (college graduates) have studied English for a good ten years. One conversation with such a person, however, will likely convince you that it was not time well spent.

What many unfortunate Japanese have for their years of English study is what one teacher succinctly calls, "inarticulate literacy." Many who've studied the language can read it exceptionally well but precious few can carry on an intelligible conversation with a native speaker. Fortunately, this means plenty of opportunity for English teachers who, the Japanese hope, can unlock the door to English for them.

Education has always been of tremendous importance in the pragmatic Japanese society but, with the Meiji Restoration of 120 years ago, Japan moved its educational efforts into high gear in a desperate attempt to catch up technologically with the rest of the world. Largely because of the country's desire to learn as much as possible about foreign technology through printed matter, a brutal form of grammar-translation was adopted for the learning of English.

With this method, the Japanese condemned themselves to almost never being able to converse with an English speaker but soon were able to read almost anything he might write. For the insular Japanese of the time, however, this suited them just fine.

After WWII, suddenly there appeared real, live English-speakers by the thousands, right there in the occupied homeland. Suddenly, the focus of English instruction needed to shift from written to spoken but change is excruciatingly slow in Japan. Nevertheless, with the conquest of their country by an English-speaking army and the perceived economic dominance of the world by that victor, the Japanese were quick to see the value of learning the language believing whole-heartedly that "if you can't beat 'em, join 'em til you can."

After having been almost banned during the war, English has grown in popularity today to such an extent that even those who could have no possible use for it study eagerly just to conform to the national mania.

Excessive as it may be, the Japanese love of English (or should we say, the love of the *learning* of English?) translates into lots of jobs for native English speakers wishing to spend time in the country. And since most of the Japanese students have had years of grammar and vocabulary instruction, schools believe that all the students really need is "conversation," however a particular school happens to interpret that rather vague catch-all term.

Most schools think conversation teachers don't really need credentials since, popular thinking goes, anyone can teach "conversation" in their native language. Teaching experience and credentials frequently aren't given as much favor in hiring in Japan as they might elsewhere and perhaps because of this, there are relatively few teachers with any sort of specific teacher training.

Largely for this reason and the fact that Japanese employers are reluctant to hire anyone sight unseen, few positions are filled from outside the country. Although it is possible to obtain sponsorship as a teacher before actually going to Japan for interviews, it is becoming more difficult as more prospective teachers are willing to go to Japan with only a tourist visa, find a sponsoring employer and then change to a working visa.

Being in Japan tells an employer some important information about you: that you are certainly serious about coming to the country, that you are probably almost over your homesickness and so will probably be fairly stable, that you probably have successfully dealt with other Japanese organizations and that he won't have to pay your airfare over. To avoid possible problems in these areas, the employer will often hire a less-qualified person locally even though a more-qualified person overseas has indicated absolute willingness to come over.

About the only way to get hired without a personal interview is to be recommended by a person (usually Japanese) whose judgement the employer trusts. Employers certainly would rather not have to interview applicants since frequently the interviewer knows nothing about teaching English and may not even speak it well himself.

Thus, endorsement by a trustworthy Japanese can sometimes do the trick--if not resulting in actual hiring before the interview then at least turning the interview into more of a confirmation. For more specific information on sponsorship and general hiring practices, please consult my general guidebook, JOBS IN JAPAN, also available from The Global Press.

In interviewing, common sense should dictate behavior and dress. Dress well and conservatively and make sure all relevant documents (resume, copies of diplomas, recommendations, photos) are in order. Be prepared to answer rather vague questions to test your sincerity such as why you came to Japan, what you think about it, and how you think Japan can best "internationalize." The successful interview will result in a contract for usually one year, possibly longer if incentives (such as return airfare) are included.

It is useful to have as your personal sponsor someone not associated with your employment. Every foreigner must have his or her stay in Japan guaranteed by an individual (it could be another "gaijin" if they've been a resident long enough) and most teachers simply let the employing school president act as theirs. Should there be some dispute about the contract you've signed with the school, however, it could be easier to extricate yourself from it if you have a totally separate person vouching for your character. Having an outside sponsor does give a bit more leverage in settling disputes with or quitting an employer.

Contracts in Japan with foreigners are generally unenforceable insofar as your ultimate out is simply to leave the country. (Don't worry, no one's ever been extradited back to Japan to face charges of classroom desertion.) The Japanese don't really like to rely on contracts either because they're never quite sure what they'll have you doing. They'd prefer to have the flexibility to ask you to do a variety of things and don't want to be limited to what is enumerated in the contract. Part-time instructors (those not given sponsorship by that school) are considered "jigyoosha" or self-employed (contract) workers, and sometimes aren't even asked to sign contracts.

Many people do indeed ignore contracts and get along fine with their employer (who often sees it as a governmental formality anyway). There is some danger, however, in breaking contract if you want to stay in the country. Anytime a "gaijin" changes employers, Immigration requires a letter of release from the former employer stating the conditions under which the foreigner left his company. (Spouses of Japanese citizens are exempt from this reporting requirement.) It's always best to be cooperative and leave an employer on terms favorable enough to get a positive Immigration letter which will allow you to change to another school.

Japan has always had a sort of love-hate relationship with the West, especially America. On the one hand, Americans are admired for their straight forwardness, independence, determination, optimism and vigor. On the other, Westerners in general are seen as willful, selfish, argumentative, and somewhat disruptive of the common good.

When Japanese return home after living abroad, one study has shown that the society at large frequently expresses concern that the returnee will be independent rather than dependent, self-reliant rather than group-cooperative, innovative rather than conforming, and responsive only to rational-legal authority rather than personal (group) authority. In short, a misfit.

For the Westerner trying to prove himself in Japan, this approval of conformity and dependence can be confusing and lead to inappropriate behavior, especially in aggressively proposing innovative ideas which the Japanese prefer to leave to senior employees. New workers (teachers or otherwise) are usually discouraged from taking an active administrative role. They are expected instead to learn how things are done traditionally, who holds power and how to avoid offending those individuals.

This, of course, can be very frustrating for the imaginative and dynamic instructor. Still, the sad truth is that schools are great believers in the expression "if it ain't broke, don't fix it." And, unfortunately, a school can be just barely surviving and still not be considered "broke" by its administrators.

Even if a new proposal is accepted, it will frequently fail because the proper channels weren't followed to ensure support among those whose participation is necessary. The Japanese will often pay "lip service" to innovation just to be agreeable but then totally neglect to follow through for successful implementation if the proper "ground work" hasn't been done.

Sociologist Chie Nakane has stated that personal loyalty is everything in Japan. Employees are expected to give undying loyalty to a single powerful figure and, for their support, they are rewarded by him. Needless to say, "office politics" run rampant in Japanese society, even, to an extent, among foreigners who are in most ways regarded as transient and ultimately expendable guest workers existing more or less outside the office sphere.

What this means for the foreigner seeking to teach in Japan is that the work environment there is an alien one and one which, after a few months of politicizing, she may not want to be actively involved in. Fortunately, the Japanese don't consider us "gaijin" as regular staff people anyway so we are largely relieved of the kind of backstage intrigues the Japanese employees are regularly embroiled in.

By far the largest number of jobs available to native English speakers involve teaching adults, usually businessmen (or, as the Japanese call them, "salaryman"). Schools offer classes in their facility or, more commonly, teachers are sent to the client company's facility to teach employees there for a charge to the company of between 8,000 and 12,000 yen per hour. These "in-company" classes with enrollments of between five and fifteen are generally held after the workday, making teaching hours between 5 and 9 p.m. Monday through Friday especially valuable.

Student, client and teacher expectations can vary dramatically with the client's goals sometimes seeming vague if not nonexistent. In one survey, for example, instructors listed their teaching goals as "activation" of past learning (i.e., helping the students recall and use what they'd learned years before in school), "unlearning" incorrect "fossilized" forms of "Japanese English," and "exposure to foreigners and their cultures."

On the other hand, companies listed their primary goal for employees learning English as being to increase the pool of employees who could use English if the need arose. Another frequently mentioned reason was to "internationalize" (although there has never been consensus on what the term means).

Many companies acknowledge that their employees are frightened of foreigners and simply would like them to learn to interact with "gaijin" without trembling with terror (I've seen it happen!). Of course, some companies with overseas operations have very real specific English needs for their employees bound for foreign assignments.

Certainly one major expectation of client companies and schools is the development of rapport between teachers and their students. Because exposure to foreigners is a major justification for the classes, it is advisable and sometimes incumbent upon teachers to socialize with their students after class, usually at a local bar or restaurant, where the teacher can be seen to be "just a regular person."

Frequently, the students' company will also invite the teacher to a weekend "retreat" at a company facility for drinking, singing and general merriment. Again, acceptance of the invitation will be strongly urged, probably by your boss who might point out (quite rightly) that it will be a lot of fun. Contrary to what many foreigners think proper behavior would be as a respected "sensei," Japanese do not expect or appreciate stuffiness or standoffish behavior from their teacher.

It is sometimes difficult for in-company teachers to plan lessons since attendance is sporadic. Employees work long, irregular hours and English classes are usually considered fairly low priority commitments, appropriate only when more immediate problems aren't pressing. When students do come, they are likely to be tired from the day's grind.

For this reason, it is usually best not to engage them in strenuous activity or assign much homework since they are probably volunteer students and wouldn't stand for more hard work after their regular work day. Pair and small-group work together with exercises allowing the student to use his own work-related knowledge are probably best for this sort of class.

Although such jobs are relatively few, it is possible to work directly for a Japanese company and not a school. One study conducted by the Sanno Institute of Business Administration in 1982 found that 75% of all foreign employees worked for manufacturing companies. Of these employees, 42% were in public relations or language resources (translation, copywriting, proof-reading, etc.) and 24% were language teachers.

Pay is comparable to a good private school but as a regular employee, the teacher is allowed full benefits which, in a Japanese company, can be considerable: health benefits, bonuses, housing allowances, sometimes even retirement plans and guaranteed employment. For these additional benefits, however, the teacher must work long hours and demonstrate the kind of unwaivering loyalty and devotion to the company that is typical of regular employees.

Because the positions are relatively few in number (most companies just don't have the need for a full-time English person) and the involvement in the Japanese work-ethic is rather daunting, first-time or visiting instructors probably shouldn't consider these positions. Too often, they place the foreigner squarely in the middle of the aforementioned maze of office politics, without even having the language skills to deal with it. Then too, before you sign on the dotted line for such a job, do be sure you've examined closely your feelings about singing the company anthem every morning at 8.

Classes in language schools proper (where students come to the schools' facilities for instruction) range in size from a handful of students to sometimes 50 or more. Many of the students will be college-age, either preparing for the difficult college-entrance examinations or seeking to graduate from their college. Other students will be housewives with little real need for English other than to impress their neighbors and feel that they're doing something useful after they've gotten their toddlers off to school.

As private enterprises started by entrepreneurs, they are unregulated and they can teach whatever they like in whatever way they choose. Consequently, no two schools are alike although many use the same texts and other materials. Although most schools are run by legitimate educators, a few are owned and operated by fast-buck artists who will take anyone with tuition to spend and pay teachers as little as possible and then only when pressured to.

To discourage student disenrollment, there is usually a hefty entrance fee charged upon enrollment in addition to monthly tuition. Some schools advance students through a program of instruction; others offer open-ended classes divided by vague levels of proficiency: beginner, intermediate and advanced.

Teachers at such schools are usually recruited either by departing teachers or through advertisements in local English newspapers, especially the Monday edition of The Japan Times. Teachers are expected to be, above all, personable and kind, the kind of person the student will want to be with even if progress is slow. Pay ranges from about 2,500 to 5,000 yen per hour with some remuneration sometimes taking the form of reduced rent in company housing, furniture, telephone, etc.

Fringe benefits, "guaranteed employment," retirement plans and medical plans are very rare (although national health insurance can usually be obtained for this last need). Duties are vague so you're advised to be sure to find out what, if anything, is expected of you in addition to teaching. Extra, unpaid responsibilities are not unusual and should be clarified before any contract is signed.

Many schools will give their teachers a guaranteed number of teaching hours for a set monthly salary with additional hours (which frequently can't be declined) being compensated at an additional rate. Better schools will keep enrollment high and teachers busy. Some smaller schools might allow enrollment to dwindle to where classes will be canceled. At this point, the teacher may be expected to help with recruitment by encouraging current students to continue their studies.

The earliest classes are special before-work sessions where salarymen try to squeeze in a little English before their work day begins. These are fairly rare and the teacher will usually be paid a premium for having to fight rush-hour trains and be at the school by, perhaps, 7:30 a.m.

Later in the morning, after the children are sent off to school, housewife classes are held until about 3 p.m. when after-school children might have their classes. Young children (8-12 years) usually come first, followed by junior high and high school students in the early evening. Adult classes with work-weary businessmen may be held until 9 or 10 p.m.

The average full-time work load of a teacher is about 20 hours per week although many more hours can be taught without too much difficulty if classes don't call for extensive travelling from one location to another. The money can be quite good but opportunities for advancement are few and job security is minimal. To balance this, however, there is always an abundance of jobs elsewhere even though your particular little school might not always be able to give you a class. Teaching

English at private schools in Japan frequently is a sort of nomadic existence.

It is theoretically possible to work and support yourself legally just by teaching private lessons on your own. Of course, you do need a Japanese citizen to act as sponsor and you might have to prove to Immigration that you have sufficient savings so that if you aren't able to attract enough students after all, you can still keep yourself from becoming a bagperson. Given that, however, it is remarkably easy to organize private classes by distributing a few well-placed flyers near your local train station and getting out the word that your English is for hire.

To be able to actually support yourself with private classes only, though, you probably would need about a year to develop the necessary connections. Most teachers use private lessons as a means of augmenting their regular paycheck from their sponsor.

All that private classes really call for are textbooks or class reading materials, a blackboard and a space large enough for five to eight students. Like at "real" schools, the teacher collects an enrollment fee (usually equal to one month's tuition) from each new student and each month, collects tuition, ordinarily about 1,500 to 2,000 yen per hour per student. Much-sought-after private classes with wealthy businessmen and professionals (usually held at coffee shops) can often pay 10,000 yen an hour and more for simple conversation. Connections provide these gems.

Although there's no denying that students are exceptionally diligent in Japan, one sometimes gets the feeling that education, as measured by ability to actually utilize what is learned, is not so important to school officials as the appearance of hard study and the memorization of voluminous quantities of data. This would certainly seem to be the case in public schools and college-level English instruction.

Japanese scholars are granted tenure as soon as they are hired by a university and it is well-known in academic circles that the scholar's job is research and, especially, publication, not instruction. In fact, the teacher who spends too much time working with students is sometimes chastized for being derelict in his scholastic duties. Evaluation is almost non-existent so the college instructor's concern for quality education is low.

Teaching is largely seen as a nuisance and one to be dispensed with as quickly as possible. Students, of course, are aware of this apathy and reflect it with large-scale absenteeism. Says one foreign college English instructor, "Neither teachers nor students, with few exceptions, expect much of themselves or each other." Not surprisingly, since graduation from university is virtually automatic (once the student is accepted based on his performance on the exceedingly difficult entrance exam), it's possible for students to go whole semesters without stepping foot on campus.

So, although university pay (between three and six million yen annually) and work schedules (sometimes as few as 90 days on campus per year) are good, there is great frustration and poor morale in store for the serious teacher. But largely because the positions are so "cushy," competition for them is severe, almost requiring a personal introduction by someone very well-connected to the hiring institution.

Again, however, due to the demoralizing atmosphere of most college English departments and the competition for the few positions, short-term teachers are not advised to apply for them. Good pay, much more fun and greater professional challenge can easily be found elsewhere, usually in the private sector.

Life for the Japanese public school student is not terribly pleasant. Made to wear severe, militaristic uniforms (wholly unflattering and roundly disliked), students are not allowed the same social development common in Western societies. There is no "senior prom" or "homecoming." Dating is not a recognized activity (although rebellious sexual activity is high) and students are expected to repress their budding social needs to prepare for that one crucial event which may well determine the shape of the rest of their lives: the college entrance examination.

English study in such an atmosphere is often bleak, consisting of long lists of vocabulary, English grammar (explained in Japanese by the teacher with the same attention to detail one would expect of a coroner) and frequent, easily-graded multiple-choice exams.

There is little discussion and rarely any vocalization of the language learned. Many students graduate from their English classes totally unfamiliar with the English sound system and, although they may actually "know" English, will regard the foreigner trying to ask directions of him in that language much as he might look at a Martian, grunting and squeaking his plea for interplanetary assistance.

In the nationally uniform Japanese school system, there exist virtually no other foreign languages but English. Some believe English in Japan serves a purpose much like Latin's in Western cultures in the last century: a good intellectual exercise, not really intended for actual use. One particularly cynical foreign high school teacher recently termed high school English instruction "an elaborate, intense rite of passage in which the more ambitious of the young people in this country demonstrate their capacity for drudgery and self-denial to the powers-that-be."

The few positions available at secondary schools are generally created by schools seeking to enhance their prestige by having a foreigner on staff. The level of English proficiency is usually very low (even among fellow Japanese English teachers), making it advisable for the teacher to have some command of Japanese, although this may not actually be required for hiring.

Classes are usually large with forty students or more, almost always at an elementary level. Additionally, students and administrators alike are often astoundingly naive about the non-Japanese world's cultures, languages and beliefs.

Although the Japanese Teacher's Union forbids hiring of full-time foreign high school instructors, interested college graduates are encouraged to apply directly to the Ministry of Education (Monbusho) in Tokyo or to The Council on International Educational Exchange, 205 E. 42nd St., New York City, NY 10017 for information on high school teaching assistantships called "Monbusho fellowships."

Partly in response to the national cry for "internationalization," more and more parents are seeking to give their wee ones a leg-up in Japan's educational rat race by having them begin their English studies at an early age. Frequently, such parents are returning from an overseas assignment where the child very quickly picked up English from friends and they seek to have him retain and develop what he's learned.

Other parents simply realize that it's best to start language habits at an early age. Ordinarily, by the time most students begin studying English in junior high school, the language has become "externalized" and can never be learned in a "natural" fashion again.

Many children's classes are organized on a casual basis by enterprising teachers in their own neighborhood. Pay is usually per child per hour and should exceed in total what the teacher is accustomed to receiving at her regular teaching job.

Six to ten students is probably an ideal size but children's classes at schools can sometimes contain as many as 30, especially in after-school "juku's" where students come to augment their school studies. When that many elementary school or even kindergarten students occupy a single room, of course, the real challenge for the teacher is trying to prevent the class from turning into utter chaos.

Working with children requires much greater energy and resourcefulness than would be necessary with older students but perhaps the rewards of having a child almost spontaneously grasp an English word or grammatical concept thanks to the teacher's repeated examples make the effort worthwhile.

A child's progress in a language is even harder to measure than an adult's. Children can almost never be taught specific linguistic items. The best the teacher can do is invent games and activities where the child is functioning in an English environment.

Pre-pubescent children are very playful and enjoy cooperative activities. They usually can't comprehend or aren't interested in abstractions (especially explanations of grammar or vocabulary) requiring the almost exclusive use of concrete objects and activities (e.g., use of the object or at least a picture of it for each vocabulary item). Most of all, they are very easily bored and distracted if they are not enjoying the activity and aren't challenged by it.

One sociologist believes that compared to their Western counterparts, Japanese kids under 8 years of age are considerably less disciplined. From 8 to 13 they seem more disciplined, although even at this age, discipline will be a problem, especially for a foreign instructor who can't express her demands to the students in Japanese. Unfortunately, schools have no concept of "combat pay" and salaries for teachers of children are comparable to those of teachers of adults.

What are realistic expectations about how much English a child can learn? Given an atmosphere of trust where the child feels safe to err, it shouldn't be too difficult to allow the young student to:

* Overcome nervousness with
foreigners
* Acquire the sounds of English
* Recognize common English
loanwords found in everyday Japanese
* Learn basic vocabulary
* Acquire basic grammar patterns

To achieve these goals alone should give any teacher a feeling of genuine accomplishment and pleasure at knowing that such a competent child, in sharp contrast to his uninitiated schoolmates, will probably always have a special affinity, fondness and talent for English.

Common Student Errors

As a rule, Japanese students almost all have the same problems, a fact which makes teaching considerably easier than having to conduct an "error analysis" of each and every student's mistakes. This is not to say that each student doesn't have difficulty with one area more than another but the problem areas are, by and large, consistent across the board.

Robert Stockwell, a UCLA linguist has termed the categories of differences between languages as "split," "new," "absent," "coalesced," "reinterpreted," and "transferred." For the Japanese student, these differences pose varying degrees of difficulty.

One of the biggest difficulties Japanese students have in pronunciation is distinguishing between two sounds (for example) where, in Japanese, there may be only one. Most Japanese couldn't hear, let alone say, the difference between "coast" and "cost." In Japanese, there's just one "o" sound. The student must learn to "split" the sounds in his mind.

Other sounds or grammatical structures (such as the articles *a, an,* and *the*) are completely absent in Japanese. These are "new." Particle markers which are common in Japanese to indicate subject, object, possessives and others are simply "absent" from English.

On the other hand, there are some differences in Japanese that the student can't merely ignore when he speaks English. Instead, he must merge such things as the special counters for certain types of objects used in Japanese (e.g., *pon* for bottles, *satsu* for books, etc.) which are "coalesced" into the simple *one, two, three* of English.

Other times, the student may recognize the function of an English structure as being similar to a Japanese structure but it's still completely different and must be "reinterpreted." For example, the English auxilliary "do" serves the same function in questions as the Japanese -ka at the end of a sentence but it is different in form. Finally (and thankfully) there are some structures such as many of the consonant sounds which can be "transferred" from Japanese to English without change.

Mistakes in vowel sounds are very common among Japanese students and may be a source of frustration for teacher and student alike. Major errors in this area are a result of either new sounds or "split" sounds. In order of difficulty, the new sounds which cause the most problems are those such as f, v, th (as in *thick*), th (as in *then*), l and r.

Problems with split sounds include the contrast between the vowel sounds in, for instance, *hit/heat, hut/hat, cat/caught/coat, suit/soot.* Among consonants, you'll find your students saying *heat* for *feet*, *za* for *the*, and *sank* for *thank*, probably because, as new sounds, they can't be heard without training.

Syntactically, students will make many mistakes as they try to transfer rules from Japanese to English. The possessive "'s" becomes an easy addition to any noun with which the Japanese would use their possessive particle "no." "Watakushi no hon" becomes "my's book."

Because there are no articles, no plural noun forms and no count or mass noun rules in Japanese, the students will apply them in English frequently at random: "those rices," "too many monies," play much game." The subjunctive is also new (in the Japanese subjunctive, there's no change in tense) so you'll hear lots of such things as, "When I was boy, my father say if I don't graduate high school, I can't take a good job."

Use of participles is in the split category as students need to differentiate between present and past participles: "I was so *exciting* when the phone rang." The passive always causes confusion too but mostly because it hasn't been drilled or explained adequately: "I was enjoyed school and I was studied hard."

For some reason, the Japanese student loves the infinitive, which is a new form for him: "She enjoyed to study with him" and "We enjoyed to see it." Paradoxically, when an infinitive would work perfectly well, many students will choose a gerund: "I was asked for washing dishes" and "Then we went to spending allowance."

Japanese is a fairly sparse language with verbs frequently omitted when the context is clear. A famous haiku poem, for instance, reads, "Mustard blossoms moon in the east; sun in the west/Old pond frog jumping water's sound." Unfortunately, some students think their English should be so uncluttered by verbs, resulting in utterances like, "He can English very well" and "He could everything at school." We can understand him perfectly well, but alas, there are certain linguistic conventions that must be observed.

Mistaken use of prepositions include *at* for *in* or *on* for *to* (and vice versa), *in* for *on* or *to*, *of* for *in*, *on* for *in*, and liberal use of *from* for just about anything. The real problem with prepositions is that the Japanese variety (*ni, e,* etc.) are usually considered part of the word they modify. For this reason, many students don't even know what a preposition is and have a hard time learning to insert them where necessary.

Articles are altogether new for the Japanese so their use is very uncertain. Oddly enough, you'll often find students overusing them in an effort to "shotgun" the sentence with so many articles that they think they're bound to get some right: "I like a fishing with the friends."

English relies primarily on placement of words to keep meaning clear--the familiar "subject, verb, direct object pattern. Word order is very flexible in Japanese, however, with word functions being defined by particles such as *wa, ga,* or *no* to let the listener know what's being said about whom.

So when your students try to speak English with the same loose rules about word placement that they're used to in Japanese, you'll probably hear some real hodgepodge arrangements like: "I must find where is my notebook," "On piano we can play," "They had white little dog," and "I like very much them." The only fixed position in a Japanese sentence is really just the final verb which always comes at the end of the sentence.

In Japanese, negation is always attached to the final verb at the end of the sentence. Consequently, negative pronouns like *no one, nobody* and *nothing* cause problems: "Everybody don't come to party," "Anybody can't speak English." And like most students of English all over the world, Japanese have difficulty with subject-verb agreement: "Some people spends too much time playing" and "Every man are hard worker."

Vocabulary says a lot about any culture, especially what is important and what is alien. The Japanese, for example, have five different words for *rice*: *ine* for the rice plant, *momi* for rice grains, *kome* for cooking rice, *gohan* for cooked rice, and *mochi* for rice cake. I've always thought it interesting too that the words for clean and pretty are identical: *kirei*.

Aside from pure rote memorization of vocabulary, English vocabulary items that cause special grief for the average student include use of *house* or *home* instead of *family*, the distinction between *come* and *go* and *bring* and *take*, and several other minor translation errors.

To intensify, we use *more*, *most* or tack -er or -est to the end of the adjective being enhanced. The Japanese pattern is to repeat the adjective to add emphasis. Consequently, Japanese will frequently say such things as, "New Year's is the big, big holiday in my country" or "I live in a little, little house."

Encourage (if not require) your students to purchase a good American or British-made English-only dictionary for use in class. Translation is rampant in most classes and is so deleterious to language learning that I forbid use of bilingual dictionaries in my classes. I think by using monolingual dictionaries, the students get the gist of the meaning just as effectively and are exposed to synonyms. They also avoid some of the outdated and just plain weird definitions that appear in Japanese English dictionaries.

Cultural differences regarding politeness can cause a fair bit of confusion. Japanese, for example, has three primary registers for talking to a superior, talking about oneself and talking to a young person or social inferior.

Sometimes the fact that we don't have special vocabulary for these registers is disquieting to the Japanese who wants to make sure he isn't inadvertently speaking to the respected teacher with vocabulary reserved for addressing the family goldfish.

This concern for politeness also manifests itself in the way Japanese respond to some yes-no questions. Whereas if a native speaker were asked "You didn't go to school today, did you?" he would probably reply (if he hadn't gone and wanted to be truthful), "No," implying "I didn't." The Japanese, on the other hand, while trying to be truthful and focusing on the speaker not the question would probably reply, "Yes," implying "You are correct. I didn't go to school." This quirk of the cultures has been cause for numerous misunderstandings and even a few false accusations. Patience, please!

Tools of the Teaching Trade

English schools in Japan generally expect their teachers to have with them a collection of exercises, drills, activities and games to be used in conjunction with textbooks and general materials provided by the school. This "bag of tricks" often serves to liven up classes and allows the teacher to avoid overreliance on the texts. Although textbooks serve as useful "points of departure" for lessons, it is the teacher's own collection of meaningful articles, exercises and "realia" (everyday artifacts) that brings an English class to life.

Getting beyond dependence on the "basic five" classroom tools of teacher, students, blackboard, classroom and textbook can be difficult in a country like Japan where the teacher is unfamiliar with the language and the means to obtain audio-visual or other supporting materials. Explaining to your school what you need and how it will benefit students, however, should encourage your Japanese supervisor to assist you in your efforts to make classes more lively and valuable.

The following activities are a few suggested ways by which you can keep your students stimulated, entertained . . . and learning.

Games should be more than relief from the usual classroom routine. They can teach every bit as effectively as a drill and much more entertainingly. With games, English is used to accomplish a task and, as such, brings students closer to the real world where the language can be used for actual communication.

You can purchase quite a number of excellent games as well. You might want to obtain catalogs of classroom aids and games from such school suppliers as Remedial Education Press, 2138 Bancroft Place NW,

Washington DC; Garrard Publishing, 1607 N. Market, Champaign, IL 61820; University of Michigan Press, Ann Arbor, Michigan; English Language Service, 5550 Wilkins Court, Rockville MD 20852 or Milton Bradley, Springfield, Mass. 01101.

The games presented here stress listening comprehension, vocabulary and communication skills (such as direction-giving). I have not included spelling games because too often these don't use the language in context. I really can't think of how a student's command of English is improved simply by coming up with as many words as possible that begin with the letter "b."

Before the game begins, the class should practice sentence patterns and vocabulary likely to be encountered playing it. Explanation of the game should be thorough and a check should be made after explaining to ensure comprehension (e.g., "So, Ellen, what happens if somebody rolls a seven?"). Competition almost always heightens student interest when teams are created.

<u>Simon Says</u> (teaches imperatives)--students are instructed to perform an overt physical response (e.g., "Put your right hand on your head") or to draw something (e.g., "Draw a large circle with a small square inside"). To teach prepositions, the teacher may present increasingly complicated commands (e.g., "Put your pencil beside your notebook which you have put under Sachie's coat.") Of course, with true "Simon Says," the student must remember to respond only when the teacher prefaces the command with "Simon says."

<u>Traveler Puzzle</u> (teaches note-taking, vocabulary, and listening comprehension)--Copies of a map showing towns, roads, railroads, a river, a lake and a mileage scale for a fictitious country are distributed to students. They are then told that a traveler must get from one point to another with only a certain amount of money or within a certain amount of time.

Students are then told about routes and transportation available and how much each costs (e.g., the train goes from town X to town Y at 50 mph and costs $20; a bicycle can be rented for travel between town Y and Mt. Gilroy for $10 a day; etc.) Students then break into small groups to figure out what combination of transportation and what route would get the traveler to his destination on time and within his budget. Careful monitoring of small group discussion is necessary to discourage use of Japanese.

<u>Crossword Puzzles</u> (vocabulary, relative clauses)-- After the concept of crosswords is explained, blank copies of the crossword are given to students and clues are given orally to colloquial words. It's best if student's names or personal activities can be worked into the activity; e.g., "Number 7 across: What Haruko eats for breakfast every morning." A good exercise for advanced students is to create their own--in English only, of course!

<u>20 Questions</u> (yes-no questions)--"It" is given a word or makes up one himself from a restricted category such as: objects in the room, any object, places, occupations, or people (living and dead). Other students then take turns asking up to 20 questions (in turn, as a group) that can only be answered yes or no, and try to guess the word. Each student may either ask a question or make a guess. Scoring is possible by giving as many points to "it" as it took questions to guess his word.

<u>Charades</u> (present continuous and simple past; vocabulary)--"It" is told or chooses his own activity and acts it out silently while the other students take turns trying to guess it using the structure being taught; e.g. "Are you (verb) + ing?" or "Did you (verb)?" You might want to form teams and time each side's efforts to add competition.

<u>Alibi</u> (past tense; reported speech)--The class is told that yesterday a bank was robbed and two suspects have been apprehended. They deny their involvement and claim to have been together at the time the crime was committed. Two volunteers from the class are then selected and told to leave the class to decide what their alibi will be.

After the remaining students have decided what questions to use in the interrogation, one "suspect" is brought back in and each student in the class asks one wh- question. The other student is then brought in and the same questions (perhaps asked by different students) are then posed. Responses are noted and all students compare them, pointing out discrepancies using reported speech; e.g., "Yoshi said they had eaten sushi but Michiko said it was chicken."

Definition (relative and noun clauses; listening)-- After the class has been divided into teams, representatives from each are given words written on pieces of paper. (Words should be of a category recently dealt with in a lesson, such as action verbs, adjectives, etc.) The team member then tries to define the word for her teammates without using the word or any of its derivatives. Time taken for the team to guess the word is recorded and the team with the least total time wins. A variation for advanced students has teams given lists of related words. Teams then try to guess as many of the words as possible within the allotted time.

Password (pronunciation)--The class is divided into teams and one student from each is sent out of the room where the teacher tells them a word. Back in class, the selected student gives one-word clues one at a time to each teammate in turn. Clues can be given only once to ensure the best possible pronunciation and can't be derivatives of the word to be guessed. As a group or individually, the team guesses the word after each clue. Score is kept by recording the number of clues necessary to guess each word with the lowest number winning.

Concentration--This game seeks to match words, either possessives with their pronouns, artifacts with occupations (hammer and carpenter), cardinal numbers with numerals, or any other relationship you can think of. On large pieces of paper, write your selection of any easily divisible number of, for example, occupational tools. Then, on index cards, write their respective occupations. Staple blank sheets over the sheets with names of tools and tape these on the board in rows and columns. Label the rows with numbers and the columns with good minimal pair letters such as b, v, f, s, m, n, etc.

Divide the class into teams. The teacher reads the word on the index card (e.g., "carpenter") and the team member must guess by calling out row and column where the corresponding tool is (e.g., a hammer). A correct guess wins another turn and that sheet from the board. Score is kept according to how many sheets each team has when the board is cleared.

<u>Picture Matching</u> (present continuous; articles)--The teacher assembles a collection of 5 to 10 similar photos or illustrations; e.g., people walking. Each student is given one without other students' seeing it and told to prepare a verbal description of it with the teacher's assistance. When all students have prepared their descriptions, each student tells his to the class. The other students take notes and remember which student said what. The photos are then mixed together and the teacher shows them one at a time to the group which then must try to match student with photo. Points may be awarded for correct guesses.

<u>Recipes</u> (articles, directions, vocabulary)--This is an especially fun game with female students but men can come up with some bizarre taste-treats too! The vocabulary of cooking is discussed with names of foods, spices and cooking techniques (such as baking, broiling, frying, etc.) presented. (Be sure the tough pronunciation items like "milk," "lard" and "flour" get included too.) The teacher puts these on the board in categories then instructs teams to choose a sufficient number from each category to make the best dishes they can (usually with a total of ten ingredients). There may be several courses. Teams then tell the class how to prepare their creation and the class votes on the tastiest or most nauseating concoction. (Be prepared for the weird!)

<u>Neighbors</u> (prepositions, vocabulary)--A rather complex game, probably best-suited for advanced students, this can be very intellectually challenging and, if you're not careful, confusing for the teacher. First, on a grid, map out the names, ages, occupations, nationalities, type of house, type of car, family size and whatever other pertinent information you can think of for about six people living in the same neighborhood. Names should be

listed vertically, the other qualifiers horizontally. Fill in each box; e.g., under Jack's family, write, "two daughters," under Nancy's car, write, "Buick."

Once the grid is completed and you understand what identity you've given each character, give blank grids to your students. After you've given a certain amount of basic information about a few grids, you can be as tricky with your descriptions as you like. For good classes, you can try "Susan is an accountant but Phil makes furniture." And later, "the carpenter [meaning Phil] lives in a townhouse." Students try to fill in all the grids with the characters' personal information.

After a few minutes of such description, you ask a deceptively easy question which is based on your long string of relationships such as "Who drives the Volvo?" Just make sure that all your relationships really have been tied together to create a "trail" leading to the answer.

<u>Map Game</u> (directions)--Two versions of a simple city map with street names and many shops and buildings are distributed to each pair of students. One version has half the shops identified, the other has the other half identified. Shops not identified are listed at the bottom of each page. Students face each other with a divider between them so the other map can't be seen.

Both students start from the same point on the map and take turns "leading" the partner to unidentified buildings by giving directions; e.g., "Now turn right on Elm St. and go up two blocks to the big tree. The pastry shop is behind the tree." First team to complete both maps wins.

<u>Drawing Game</u> (shapes)--Discuss vocabulary of shapes: squares, rectangles, cubes, etc. Students are paired and each student is given one of two versions of a collection of five composite shapes; e.g., a square in a circle above a triangle. As in <u>Map Game</u>, students face each other with a divider. Each student must describe the shapes on his paper to his partner without gesturing until his partner thinks he's got it. After each student has described to his partner all five shapes, the class examines each team's efforts and names the most accurate reproductions as winners.

Grid Games (directions, prepositions)--The Drawing and Map games obviously are similar in that students must describe what they see effectively enough for their team mate to approximate what is being described. Such games are often played on grids (pieces of paper, lined off into boxes) wherein players will arrange photos, drawings or even small objects, then describe that placement to their team mates so that an accurate description is possible.

A variation of this is to give the students two sets of objects and have them use their whole desk as a grid, placing objects in corners, on their sides, on top of one another, etc. In this case, its's probably wise to have students sit with their backs to each other, rather than relying on a simple paper divider between them.

Debate--Students are told to think of an individual living or dead whom they think is the most important person in the world. The students are then told that all these people are passengers in a dropping balloon and all but one must jump out. Each student must defend for one minute why his choice should be the only person to survive. Students then vote for someone other than their own choice to decide the winner.

Interview--Students are assigned three to a team and told to decide what famous person (living or dead) one of them would like to be. The other two team members act as interviewers of the celebrity. Allow about ten minutes for students to prepare their interview, then have them perform for the class. The class may vote on which celebrity they would like to have back for next week's show.

Gossip (reported speech)--Best if desks can be arranged in a circle but workable with conventional seating. Teacher works from a list of ten sentences demonstrating a recent teaching point; e.g., present progressive. One at a time, he whispers them to the first student who whispers them to the second, and so forth; e.g., "I'm eating a ripe red tomato. He's listening to an old Beatles record." A 30-second pause should be allowed between whispers to allow for "bottlenecks." The last student the whispers the utterance back to the teacher who notes what he hears next to what he originally said. Comparison of the two makes for pretty good hilarity.

Bingo (numbers; pronunciation)--Students should take turns calling the numbers, which should be quite large to exercise the Japanese student's confusion with thousands and ten thousands (which, in Japanese, is a separate category called "man"). Also, rather than b, i, n, g and o being used, vary the row letters according to pronunciation needs: f, s, b, v, e (which students may pronounce "a"), i (which may come out "e"), n, m, etc. Although it may seem odd to have students call out "V 13,000," they'll get more out of that kind of game than what we're used to at home. An alternative, of course, is just to pick up a kid's bingo game at a game store.

Pronunciation can be difficult to teach due to its usually being presented in isolation without any meaningful context. Especially for Japanese students with their "impoverished" system of far fewer sounds than those commonly used in English, however, it is essential.

In instruction, the teacher usually first models the correct sound, then explains in simple terms how the sound can be made and where the various speech organs are to be placed in the mouth. ("No, I'm not kidding. You really *do* need to put your tongue between your teeth.") The students then practice making the sound in isolation, in a word and with the word in a sentence. Individuals and the group as a whole try it with the teacher making corrections as needed.

It's best to teach pronunciation with "minimal pairs," that is, similar sounds which students frequently confuse. Such minimal pairs could be b/v, th/s, p/b, d/g, z/d, sh/ch or l/r. One popular minimal pair drill is having the teacher stand behind the students in the back of the class and say one of the minimal pair words which the students then have to guess by holding up one finger or two. Students can then be paired off to see if their partner can guess which *they're* trying to say.

But rather than just having the students practice *"thick/sick"* a few dozen times, it's far better to try to contextualize the exercise by making either choice of the pair meaningful. One exercise to do this is to create two scenarios dependent on the minimal pair. For example, explain to the class the concept of "stealing a base." Then write on the board and teach them the phrase "He's stealing a base for his team." Next teach them "He's stealing a vase for his house." Write this on the board and have the students work with the different sounds.

Then move to the back of the room where the students can't see you and call the students to the front of the class one by one to face you. You then signal which sound you want the student to say (either b or v) by raising one finger or two. The student then says the appropriate opening phrase, "He's stealing a base" or "He's stealing a vase" and the students respond with the completion, "for his team" or "for his house." This gives meaning to the distinction between the sounds and makes the students realize just how subtle but important that difference can be.

"Realia" is becoming increasingly popular in the ESL/EFL classroom as teachers strive to bring more pieces of the real world into their language classes. By definition, "realia" can be any prop or artifact one would ordinarily encounter in the "real world."

Most language teachers tend to have the following as their basic "tool kit": a large calendar for teaching dates and tenses, large maps or a globe to teach directions and country names, crossword and picture puzzles, a large clock with movable hands to teach time, menus (many restaurants will supply you with a set of these before you go), tableware for dining etiquette instruction, a collection of clothing, post office materials, magazine and newspapers for current events, travel posters and brochures, food packages, a large paper thermometer for temperatures and weather, foreign money to practice giving and getting change, mirrors for pronunciation instruction, and motor vehicle department booklets for sign and direction practice. Any item you encounter that you think would help illustrate your instruction should certainly be brought to class.

If you'd like to invest a little money in "tools," you might want to purchase a "teletrainer" before you begin teaching in Japan. Basically, this device is just a set of two telephones with long cords and a control box which produces a ring or busy signal. The conversation on the line can be private or broadcast over a speaker to the whole class. Students using the teletrainer should be placed so they can't see each other and use facial expressions or gestures.

Sometimes, your local phone company will give or loan a teletrainer to you. Otherwise, you can probably find one through a teaching supply company. If the expense is too great, you could take all the necessary ordering information to your Japanese boss and try to persuade him to buy one for the school. A cheap alternative is get a simple intercom system, such as those sold by "Radio Shack."

Exercises with the teletrainer might include asking about store hours, when a film starts, product availability, making a business appointment, cancelling an appointment and the ever-popular calling in late to work.

Although more reserved teachers and students sometimes are a bit inhibited performing, songs really are an enjoyable classroom activity, especially with children and young adult students. Because the melody and lyrics are interwoven, retention of words seems heightened and certain structures can be very effectively presented in an entertaining way. You can almost always find someone in the class who plays the guitar and encourage him to bring it to class one day.

When selecting a song for class, be sure it has value in either grammar, pronunciation, vocabulary or culture. The tune should be simple and easily remembered. Lyrics should be repetitive with the chorus being especially easy to learn. Make sure the lyrics are standard English, not unusual slang or antiquated. Stick to conservative songs with simple messages--remember the song is for language learning, not cosmic profundity.

When presenting a song, it's best to first introduce it by giving a bit of its history as well as background on who wrote it, then pass out copies of the lyrics or write them on the blackboard. (You might also consider leaving out a few words which the students will have to catch in the song.) Then sing or play the song through completely and read the lyrics out loud to the class, discussing any vocabulary or grammar points with them.

Have the class practice the chorus first, then the verses, one by one. Always model each verse yourself before asking the students to try it. Finally, sing the whole song through as a group several times and, if anyone in the class is an accomplished singer, invite him or her to give a solo performance.

Some traditional ESL/EFL songs include "Bingo" (teaches individual letter sounds), "Michael Row the Boat Ashore" (teaches the imperative, l, r, s and h sounds) "Oh Susanna" (simple past tense), "I've Been Working on the Railroad" (present perfect continuous tense and *can't*), "Red River Valley" (simple present, future and present tenses; modals *may* and *would*; sounds l, r, and th) and "The Drunken Sailor" (modal *shall*; sounds l, r, and sh). You'll find these and more in music store songbooks or at the library.

Teaching English in Japan is one of life's true joys, I believe. It's not very often that we have the opportunity to share something of ours with another human being who genuinely admires and values it. Such a gift is the English we give Japanese students, probably the best motivated learners of our language on the planet. By organizing our teaching efforts, we can benefit them in a very real and meaningful way and, not incidentally, allow ourselves to experience their delightful country which they seem to so enjoy sharing with us.

To be the best teacher possible in Japan's English classrooms, try to decide which method best suits your style and your students' needs. Bring some good non-text related materials with you to lend a little variety to your classes (especially games, pronunciation charts and "realia"). Familiarize yourself with the problems your students are likely to have, then decide how best to treat them.

Discourage translation, either spoken or in thought. Make your students respond quickly to your questions so they'll start *thinking* in English and not perform the usual

"English question-to-Japanese question-to-Japanese thought-to-Japanese answer-to-English answer" process which can kill precious class time and probably drive you (and the other students) up the wall.

Keep your classes lively and laugh a lot. Studies have actually shown that humor is very beneficial in helping a student grasp a foreign language. Certainly it builds rapport and trust with the teacher.

You must honestly like your students and be curious about their lives. Encourage their efforts and emphasize to them how difficult Japanese is for you so they won't feel quite so discouraged when they make the same mistakes over and over.

Above all, have fun and enjoy your students' company. Try not to take on so many hours that students' faces all start to blur into a single mass of humanity before you. If you feel that happening, pull back--you're starting to burn out. If you pace yourself right and teach because you honestly want to share your language with people who sincerely want to learn it, you're guaranteed to have a thoroughly enjoyable and satisfying time teaching in Japan.

APPENDIX: SAMPLE LESSON PLAN

Estimated Time of Lesson: 30 minutes

Teaching Point: "he" and "she"

How Need Determined: frequent student errors with "he" and "she"

Relevance to Current Unit: related possessive pronoun lesson in current chapter

Earlier Instruction: taught in Chapter 3 but a refresher seems needed

Performance Objectives: to have students see difference between "he" and "she"

Materials: woman's hat and man's hat

Procedure: (Step 1: Introduction): teacher models pattern pronoun, occupation and attribute; e.g.,"Tanaka-san is a banker. He's a rich man." (Step 2): teacher gives hat to male or female student and states occupation (e.g., grocer). Other student gives pattern, "Oishi-san is a grocer." Another student is selected to complete with attribute (e.g., "He's a healthy man.") (Step 3): teacher switches hats so that male students are given the woman's hat and so must be referred to as "she."

Contingency Plans: If students seem rather uneasy about the sex role switch, use well-known Japanese celebrities.

Post-lesson Evaluation: students seemed to enjoy the role reversal and the need to think up attributes. Very lively lesson.

APPENDIX: SUGGESTED CLASSROOM NAMES

The following names have been chosen as appropriate for classroom use because each has within it some pronunciation problem for the Japanese student. It is advisable to briefly mention to students that their "English names" are just for fun and to help them practice pronunciation, become familiar with foreign names and make it easier for them to develop an English-speaking identity.

MEN: Aaron, Abel, Abner, Abraham, Adair, Adlai, Adrian, Alan, Albert, Alexander, Alexander, Alfred, Alger, Alvin, Andrew, Ansel, Anthony, Arlen, Arnold, Arthur, Averill, Avery, Barry, Barton, Bernard, Bert, Bill, Brandon, Brett, Brian, Broderick, Bruce, Burgess, Burton, Byron, Calder, Calvin, Cameron, Carey, Carl, Cecil, Charles, Christopher, Clarence, Claude, Clifford, Clyde, Colin, Craig, Curtis, Dale, Daniel, Darrell, David, Dennis, Derrick, Donald, Dorian, Drake, Drew, Douglas, Edgar, Edward, Elijah, Elliot, Elmer, Elton, Elvis, Elwood, Emery, Eric, Ernest, Erwin, Everley, Farley, Farrell, Felix, Ferdinand, Flynn, Francis, Frank, Gabriel, Gardner, Gerald, Gerard, Giles, Glenn, Gordon, Gregory, Halsey, Harlan, Harley, Harold, Harris, Harry, Harvey, Henry, Herbert, Herman, Hilary, Hiram, Holmes, Holt, Horace, Howard, Hubert, Humphrey, Irving, Jarvis, Jeffrey, Jerome, Julius, Kelly, Kermit, Killian, Kirby, Lambert, Lawrence, Leonard, Lester, Lionel, Lloyd, Luke, Luther, Lyndon, Malcolm, Mark, Marshall, Marvin, Melvin, Merle, Milo, Mitchell, Mortimer, Murray, Noel, Norton, Oliver, Orville, Palmer, Patrick, Perry, Ralph, Randolph, Riley, Roland, Ronald, Rudolph, Rupert, Samuel, Saul, Sterling, Theobald, Theodore, Tracy, Truman, Verne, Vernon, Victor, Vincent, Virgil, Walter, Walton, Warner, Wilbur, Wilfred, William.

WOMEN: Abigail, Adelaide, Adelle, Aileen, Alice, Alva, Andrea, Angelica, Annabelle, April, Arlene, Athena, Audrey, Aurora, Avis, Barbara, Belle, Bernice, Bertha, Beryl, Beth, Beverly, Blythe, Brenda, Camille, Cara, Carla, Carol, Caroline, Cathleen, Celeste, Charlotte, Clara, Clarissa, Claudia, Coral, Crystal, Cynthia, Darlene, Deborah, Delilah, Dolores, Doris, Dorothy, Edith, Eleanor, Electra, Elizabeth, Ella, Emily, Erma, Estelle, Esther, Eulalia, Evangeline, Evelyn, Faith, Fern, Florence, Frances, Gail, Gertrude, Gladys, Gloria, Harriet, Heather, Irene, Judith, Kelly, Kimberly, Laraine, Laura, Lena, Leslie, Lillian, Luella, Lynn, Martha, Melissa, Millicent, Miriam, Moira, Muriel, Myrna, Norma, Olga, Ophelia, Pamela, Paula, Phyllis, Priscilla, Rachel, Rochelle, Ruth, Samantha, Scarlett, Sheila, Shirley, Tabitha, Thelma, Valerie, Verna, Veronica, Victoria, Virginia, Vivian, Wilhemina.

APPENDIX: SELECTED REFERENCE BOOKS

1. Brown, H. Douglas; Principles of Language Learning and Teaching; Prentice-Hall.

2. Brownell, John; A Directory of Resources for the Study of English in Japan; University Press, University of Hawaii.

3. Celce-Murcia, Marianne; Teaching English as a Second or Foreign Language; Newbury House.

4. Dixson, Robert; Practical Guide to Teaching English as a Foreign Language; Regents.

5. Dubin, Fraida and Elite Olshtain; Facilitating Language Learning; McGraw-Hill.

6. Frank, Marcella; Modern English: A Practical Reference Guide; Prentice-Hall.

7. Gordon, Douglas; Communicating in Japanese--A Tactical Approach; Sci-Trans Press, PO Box 9302, Denver CO 80209.

8. Jolly, Constance and Robert; When You Teach English as a Second Language; Book Lab.

9. Kimizuka, Sumako; Teaching English to Japanese; Neptune Books.

10. Leatherdale, C.; So You Want to Teach English to Foreigners; International School Book Service.

11. Martins, Samuel; Basic Japanese Conversation Dictionary; Tuttle & Co.

12. Oller, John; Methods That Work; Newbury House.

13. Praninskas, Jean; Rapid Review of English Grammar; Prentice-Hall.

14. Rivers, Wilga; A Practical Guide to the Teaching of English; Oxford University Press.

15. Savill-Troke, Muriel; Foundations for Teaching English as a Second Language; Prentice-Hall.

16. Stevick, Earl; Teaching Languages---A Way and Ways; Newbury House.

17. Wattenberg, Beverly; A Guidebook for Teaching English as a Second Language; Allyn Publishers.

18. Wellman, Laurie; License Examination Review for Teachers of English as a Second Language; Arco.

19. Wharton, John; JOBS IN JAPAN--The Complete Guide to Living and Working in the Land of Rising Opportunity; Global Press.

20. Wordell, Charles B.; A Guide to Teaching English in Japan; *Japan Times*.

21. Yamamoto, Mitsu; Bridges to Fear; Newbury House.

APPENDIX: QUICK GUIDE TO GRAMMAR

(Taken from <u>A Rapid Review of English Grammar</u> by Jean Praninskas. See this book for further explanations and classroom exercises.)

The following description of English grammar represents a good sequencing of grammatical structures for presentation to students of the language. A student's level of proficiency can also be judged somewhat by determining what structures he or she is proficient with. All structures mentioned before that "outer limit" of proficiency should be fairly well mastered before more advanced grammar is introduced.

"Be" verb:

An irregular verb which changes depending on person and number: Singular: 1st=I am, 2nd=You are, 3rd=He/She/It is; Plural: 1st=We are, 2nd=You are, 3rd=They are.

Used for occupations, nationality, age, characteristics, condition, size or shape, color or place.

Placed at the beginning of the sentence to form yes-no questions.

Past tense: *was/were* depending person and number.

Follows wh- words in information questions that ask *who* (person), *what* (thing), *where* (place), *when* (time) or *why* (reason).

Used with nominative pronouns *I, you, he/she/it, we, they.* Such pronouns require a referant person or thing before use.

Can be contracted using apostrophes to indicate missing letters in *I'm, you're, he's/she's/its, we're, they're, that's, who's, what's, where's, here's, there's.*

Can be negated into *isn't, wasn't, aren't, weren't.*

Demonstratives:

This (singular) and *these* (plural) refer to objects close to the speaker.

That (singular) and *those* (plural) refer to objects some ways from speaker.

May be used in noun position or as adjectives before nouns.

Place words:
Here indicates the speaker's location. *There* indicates a place which can be pointed to or which has been previously mentioned.

Articles:
Most singular nouns are preceded by *a* if the following word begins with a consonant sound and *an* if the following word begins with a vowel sound.
The is used for singular nouns and indicates a specific item, as contrasted with the more general *a*.

Names and Titles:
No title is used before a given name if the family name is not mentioned.
A man may be called *Mr.* when his given and last names are mentioned or only his last name. He may also sometimes be called by his last name without his title but this is considered very informal and sometimes crude.
A woman may be called *Mrs.* with either her husband's or her own given name and usually her husband's last name. On legal documents, she must use her given name. Many modern women prefer to hyphenate their maiden (unmarried) name and their husband's name or, in some cases, use her maiden name only even after she has married. Single women usually use the title *Miss* although some women today, both married and single, use *Ms.* to avoid having their marital status identified.

Simple present tense:
Doesn't actually express present activity (present progressive does that). Used to express repeated, customary, habitual actions and general truths.
When used with a future time expression (word, phrase or clause), indicates that it is a forthcoming event; e.g. "Sadahiro graduates in June."

Auxiliary "do":

Usually added to sentence before verb to make negative statements or at beginning of sentence to form yes-no questions. As an auxiliary, it has no meaning of its own and is purely functional. Not to be confused with the meaningful *do* which means "act upon."

Does used in third person singular (he/she/it).

Contracted negative forms: *don't, doesn't.*

Follows wh- words for informational questions; e.g., "Where do you ski?"

May serve as "pro-verb" also if action is unknown; e.g. "What do you do on weekends?"

Used in American English with have but not in British English; e.g., American: "Doesn't he have a pencil?"; British: "Hasn't he a pencil?"

S-forms (-s):

Used after singular nouns and demonstratives and after pronouns he, she, it. Simple forms without -s are used in all other cases. Object pronouns:

Receives the action in a sentence; e.g., "She kissed me."

Singular: 1st person=me, 2nd=you, 3rd=him/her/it; Plural: 1st=us, 2nd=you, 3rd=them.

It is used for ships and countries (except in literature) and babies and animals when the sex is unknown.

Whom is seldom used in conversation except when it directly follows a preposition; e.g., "For whom do the bells toll?" More common and acceptable would be, "Who do the bells toll for?" Both are correct.

Compound sentences:

And joins two affirmative statements; e.g., "Bill eats downtown and watches the people." Unrelated statements cannot be joined by *and.*

But joins contrasting statements, both affirmative and negative; e.g., "Bill eats downtown but shops at the mall."

Semicolon (;) is used to join two simple statements instead of *and* or *but*; e.g., "Bill eats downtown; he shops at the mall." A comma must never be used this way.

Phrases:

A group of words which function together as a unit to perform a single function, filling a position in a sentence pattern.

Does not have a subject and related verb.

Prepositional phrases:

Usually introduced by a preposition, especially when describing a place; e.g. in a library, at the movies.

Two or more place phrases may be used together; e.g., on a table down the hall. Usually appear at the end of a sentence but may be placed at the beginning for emphasis, generally with the expletive *there*; e.g., "At the park, there are swans."

Verbs of motion (go, walk, etc.) are often followed by place phrases beginning with *to*; e.g., "I'll go to the park." Some places require use of *to*, and article and the place. Others don't require the article; e.g. "We go to school." Still others (such as home and downtown) require neither; e.g., "You go home."

Time phrases are similar to place phrases and take prepositions *in, at,* and *on*; e.g. "in the morning," "at noon," and "on Sundays." (The -s with Sunday idicates a habitual action.) Usually appear at the end of a sentence but may also be placed at the end for emphasis. Time phrases with every do not use a preposition; e.g., "every Sunday."

Two-word verbs:

Phrases consisting of a verb and a particle (preposition or adverb) which changes the meaning of the verb. The two words function together and cannot be taken seperately without changing the meaning of the verb; e.g., get up (from bed).

Voiced / voiceless sounds:

Voiced sounds are made with the vocal cords vibrating, voiceless without; e.g., *f, p, t,* and *k.* All vowels are voiced and half of all consonants.

Continuous present tense:

Also called present progressive.

Formed by joining present form of auxiliary *be* plus a simple verb plus an ing-form.

Used to express action occurring in immediate present ("I am eating") or for actions or conditions during a period of time including the present; e.g., "He's studying English this month."

May also be used to indicate a forthcoming event; e.g., "He's graduating in June."

When used in yes-no questions, contracted form is almost always used; e.g., "Aren't you going to school?" The uncontracted form is more formal and requires the not to be placed directly before the ing-form; "Are you not going to school?"

Usually reserved for action verbs. Non-action verbs which express mental states or conditions and verbs of perception don't usually use continuous present; e.g., believe, know, seem, understand, like, love, need, prefer, want, wish, remember, forget, belong, own, owe, cost, mean, resemble, hear, see.

Ing-forms:

Depending on function, also called present participle, gerund, verbal, verbal noun, verbal adjective.

Spelling rules when adding -ing: when simple verb ends in *e,* drop *e* before adding ing. When one-syllable verb ends in a single consonant, preceded by single vowel (e.g., stop), double consonant before adding -ing (e.g., stopping). If preceded by two vowel (e.g., look) do not double consonant (e.g., looking).

Never functions alone as a verb; e.g. "I trying to study." Always requires the auxiliary be in one of its conjugated forms (e.g., is, am, are).

Expletive "there":

Not an adverb denoting a place, in this usage, it is a word which means nothing but calls attention to whatever is referred to in the rest of the sentence.

Usually followed by *be* verb.

Agrees in number (singular or plural) with subject which follows it.

Usually requires a place expression for completion; e.g. "There are two books on the table." A place expression is required even if it is the place "there"; e.g., "There's a book there."

Sentence pattern is normal if there refers to a place already mentioned; e.g., "There a student can study freely." Sentence pattern is inverted if there refers to something being pointed to; e.g., "There is my book." *Here* functions the same way.

Possessive pronouns:

May either modify nouns (e.g., my, your, his/her/its, our, their) or be used in place of nouns; e.g., mine, yours, his/hers/its, ours, theirs.

When used in place of nouns, they must refer to something recently mentioned; e.g., "That book is mine. Where's yours?"

Whose is the possessive form of *who*. It usually appears directly before a noun; e.g. "Whose dog is this?" It can also be used by itself but only if the items possessed are in sight and indicated; e.g. "Whose is this?"

Frequency Adverbs:

Used to express approximately how often a customary or habitual action or condition is repeated.

Not usually used with continuous tenses; e.g. is going.

Includes (in declining frequency): Affirmatives: always, usually frequently, often, sometimes, occasionally. Negatives: seldom, rarely, hardly ever, never. Interrogative: Ever?

Immediately precede the verb in simple statements unless verb is *be* in which case they follow; "He often calls his mother," "He is always concerned." Sometimes also may appear at sentence beginning and end.

Affirmative forms used to negate with *not*. Negative forms alone also negate; e.g. "He doesn't often forget." "He seldom forgets."

Numbers:

Cardinal numbers are used in counting and reckoning (math).

Ordinal numbers indicate rank; e.g., "first place."

When a noun is modified by both a cardinal and ordinal number, the ordinal number comes first; e.g. "The first ten days of school are the most difficult."

Dates are written with cardinal numbers but pronounced as ordinal; e.g., "July 4, 1776" is read, "July fourth, seventeen seventy six."

Prepositions with times, dates and places:

In is used before months, years, seasons, special time expressions (e.g., "in the evening"), continents, countries, states, cities and towns.

On is used before days of the week, dates, and streets.

At is used before the time of day, special time expressions (e.g., "at night") and numbers of buildings (e.g., "He lives at 2728 Elm St.")

Transitive/intransitive verbs:

Transitive verbs are those verbs that take an object and are frequently action verbs; e.g. "He hit the ball."

Intransitive verbs are frequently "state of being" verbs; e.g., "He lives in Tokyo."

Countables and uncountables:

Uncountables are words for things which cannot be counted; e.g. weather.

Countables must be preceded by *a* or *an* for the singular. Uncountables have no plural forms and can never be preceded by *a* or *an*.

There are four categories of uncount-ables: abstract (e.g., advice, help, information, knowledge, trouble, work, enjoyment, fun, recreation, relaxation), material (e.g., meat, rice, bread, cake, coffee, water, oil, grass, hair), generic (e.g., fruit, equipment, furniture, mail luggage, jewelry, clothing, money) and non-plurals with final -s (e.g., economics, mathematics, mumps, measles, news, tennis).

A little and *some* are used before uncountables to indicate a small quantity.

Much may be used to indicate large quantities but is mainly used in negative statements and questions; e.g., "Do you have much work?"

A few is used before plural countables in affirmative statments and questions to indicate a small amount.

Many may be used before all plural countables to indicate a large quantity.

Of follows many, much, a few, a little and some when the nouns they modify are identified; e.g., "Many of my best friends are the students I teach."

Quantity terms used with both uncountables and plurals: *some* (not usually used in negative statements), *any* (used in negative statments but does not make it negative; e.g., "I don't use any sugar"), *a lot/lots of*, *no* (indicates an absence; e.g. no charge. *Quite* reverses the meaning of these; e.g. "quite a few"= many. *Any* is also used to mean it doesn't matter which or who; e.g., "Any tourist may enter Osaka castle."

Verbs used with uncountables are always singular. Pronouns which substitute for uncountables are also singular; e.g. "Virtue is its own reward."

Some words may be either countable or uncountable with different meaning depend-ing on which is used; e.g., change (alteration or money), glass (receptacle or material), youth (young person or being young).

Irregular plural countables: feet, teeth, mice, men, women, children, oxen.

Some Greek and Latin countables have their original plurals; e.g., analyses, bases, crises, data, phenomena, stimuli, formulae, media, memoranda.

No plural form exists for: deer, fish, or sheep.

Names of some things composed of two similar parts are always plural; e.g., scissors, tweezers, tongs, trousers, pants, pajamas, glasses, spectacles, binoculars.

Reflexive pronouns:

Used with some verbs to emphasize that the subject and object have the same referent; e.g., "We enjoyed ourselves."

Used to emphasize that the verb was performed by the subject and not another agent; "She made lunch herself."

When preceded by *by*, it means alone ("Hiroo studies by himself.") or without assistance; e.g., "He did all the homework by himself."

Idioms with "go":

Go +ing form of verb is used for active recreation; e.g. go fishing, go dancing, go skiing.

Simple future tense:

Formed with either *be* + going to + simple verb; e.g., "Haruko is going to have a party" or with *will* + simple verb; e.g. "Haruko will have a party."

Will + simple verb also may suggest promise, determination or inevitability.

For reference to immediate future (just after speaking), use *be* + about to + simple verb; e.g., "Haruko is about to serve the ice cream."

Continuous future:

Formed with *will* + *be* + ing form; e.g., "Jack will be helping Haruko at her party."

Used to emphasize an ongoing activity at a very specific time in the future which must be referenced in the sentence or very recently in another sentence.

Future time expressions:

May be formed with words (e.g., soon, later, tomorrow); pharases (e.g., next (week), in (a minute), (a week) from now [end of phrase only], the (day) after (tomorrow), at (noon); or clauses (groups of words which function as units in a sentence).

Clauses are introduced by "clause markers" (e.g., where, when, who) which indicate a clause beginning. Clauses also have subjects which can sometimes be the clause marker; e.g., "Everyone who sees Kyoto wants to stay."

Time clauses are introduced by when; "He will answer when you call." They may also appear at the beginning of the sentence; e.g., "When you call, he will answer." Time clauses always take -s form verbs (present tense), never future verbs with will or going.

"Then":

Can be a time word refering to a time previously mentioned. Usually comes at the end of a sentence; e.g., "Kimiko will be in class then."

Can also be a sequence signal, like next, at the beginning of a sentence; e.g., "First Pat will eat lunch. Then she'll study."

Then is not a connective to join sentences but is frequently joined by a connective; e.g., "First Pat will eat lunch and then she'll study."

Indefinite "you" and "they":

In this sense, *you* means anyone or everyone in a colloquial expression; e.g., "You never know."

They refers to an indefinite body of experts or popular opinion; e.g., "They say the price of oil will rise."

Possessives:

Not all nouns have possessive forms. If not, *of* must be used; e.g. "legs of the table."

Nouns with possessive forms include persons, animals, places, times, and money (when followed by worth); e.g., "five dollars worth of gas."

When the base form ends in s, form the possessive by adding an apostrophe. Otherwise, add apostrophe s.

Adjective phrases:

Consist of a preposition, noun and other modifiers.

Occurs after word it modifies; e.g., "A boy with green shoes." Single word adjectives occur before the word; e.g., "A tall boy..."

The verb of the sentence agrees in number with the subject noun not with the noun in the adjective phrase; "That book of wonderful stories about kings, queens, knights and dragons is great!"

When the adjective phrase limits the meaning of the modified noun to one possibility, the noun is preceded by *the*; e.g., "The men in that car are suspicious."

Simple past tense:

Expresses a one-time completed past event; "Yasuo saw Mary."

Regular past tense forms end in -ed. The approximately 150 irregular forms must be memorized because they are not predictable.

Irregular forms are made by: leaving same as present (e.g., split, bet), final consonant change (built, spent), vowel and consonant change (brought, taught), vowel changes (bleed=bled, spin=spun, find= found).

In sentences which require use of auxiliaries, past tense is applied to the auxiliary, not the main verb; e.g., "Did Hideo walk to school yesterday?"

Ago is used only with simple past tense and appears at the end of the time phrase. It refers to a specific time, counting back from the present; e.g., "Bill sold his car a week ago."

Before and *after* express a simple sequence relationship; e.g., "Bill sold his car before he moved."

While emphasizes the passage of time and simultaneous action; "Kazuko slept while the teacher lectured." *Frequently* used with continuous tenses (-ing form verbs) because of duration; e.g., "While the teacher was lecturing, Kazuko slept."

When can refer to punctual action; e.g., "Where were you when I fell down?"

Was/were going to + simple verb:
Expresses unfulfilled plans.

Often followed by but and an independent clause (one with subject and verb) explaining why the plan was abandoned; e.g., "Ted was going to watch TV but he fell asleep."

"One of":
Introduces a noun phrase which includes a plural noun.

The plural noun is always modified; e.g., "one of my students."

When the "one of" phrase is the subject of a clause, the verb form is singular. It agrees with one; e.g., "One of the boys was late."

The possessive *of* is used to avoid ambiguity; e.g., "at the home of one of my friends."

None of is similar but it requires the verb to agree with noun following *of* if the phrase is the subject of a clause; e.g., "None of the teachers want to grade homework."

"In, on, at" (continued):

In indicates the position of something surrounded; e.g., "in the library."

On indicates contact with a surface; e.g., "on the table."

At indicates proximity; e.g., "the girl at the window."

Used to + verb:

Expresses past custom, habit or repeated action which no longer occurs; e.g., "I used to study Japanese."

Questions and negatives are formed with the auxiliary *do* as in the simple past.

Any more:

An adverbial expression used in negative statements and questions indicating that a condition or situation which previously existed no longer exists; e.g., "I don't study Japanese any more."

Have to + verb:

Expresses necessity. Uses auxiliary *do* for questions and negatives; "Do you have to go home now?"

May be affirmative (e.g., "We have to eat every day"), negative ("But people who fast don't have to eat every day"), yes-no questions (e.g., "Do we have to study every day?") or information questions (e.g., "When do we have to leave for the show?")

Expletive "it":

In this sense, *it* fills a position in the sentence and doesn't refer to anything; e.g., "It won't take long to finish."

May be used as impersonal *it* for weather, time, distance and identification (e.g., "Who is it?")

Very, too, enough:

Very is an intensifier which strengthens the word which immediately follows; "Debbie was very kind." Precedes the word it modifies.

Too does not intensify and is more specific than very. Used when an action is impossible because of the condition following too; "It was too nice outside to work."

Sometimes used for great difficulty rather than impossibility; e.g., "He talks too fast to understand." Precedes the word it modifies.

Enough means a sufficiency. Used when the infinitive after *enough* is made possible by the situation before enough; "Ken was smart enough to go to Stanford." Follows the word it modifies. Infinitives are units with *to* and a simple verb (e.g., to go).

Duration:

Duration of a condition or activity may be expressed with *for* and *until.*

For introduces a phrase. Often followed by a cardinal number or *a;* "for seven days."

Until introduces a phrase or clause. The time stated indicates the end of the duration period; "Jim works until five o'clock."

Continuous past tense:

Formed by a verb phrase made of a past form of *be* and an -ing form; e.g., was walking. Patterns are same as those of continuous present.

Sometimes called past progressive tense.

Requires use with expression of specific time (either in sentence or recently referred to in earlier sentence). Time expression may occur at the beginning or end of the sentence; e.g., "Jeff was painting his apartment all day."

Frequently used with *while.*

Compound sentences:

Two whole, complete sentences joined together by a connective (e.g., and, but, etc.) to form one sentence with different subjects but only one predicate (verb).

The second predicate is reduced to the first auxiliary of the verb phrase in continuous tenses (be + -ing form); e.g., "Claire was reading a book and Jack was too." (Reading is implied for Jack's action.)

Do is used instead of the auxiliary if the first verb is in simple present or past form; e.g., "Hiroshi studies hard and Jun does too." *Do* is also used to replace *used to* and *have to*; "Julie had to leave early and Louise did too."

Too is used when statements are affirmative; *either* is used for negative statements; e.g., "Claire didn't leave the library and Jack didn't either."

So and *neither* may be used instead of *too* and *either* but must be placed immediately following the connective and cause the word order of the second clause to be inverted; e.g., "Tony didn't visit Korea and neither did Karen."

Each/every/all:

Each focuses on the seperate members of a group; e.g., "Each student must submit a report."

Every, emphasizes the unity and commonality of the group; e.g., "Every student wants to do well."

All stresses completeness and finali-ty. It is used before plurals and uncountables. The verb form agrees with the noun which follows *all*; e.g., "All [of] the flowers were displayed beautifully." (Of is optional.)

Not all means part; e.g., "Not all the florists displayed their works."

"One" as a non-number:

May be an indefinite personal pronoun meaning any or every person. Rather formal and usually used only in writing; e.g., "One must be diligent."

May be used to avoid repetition of lengthy noun phrases; e.g., "Our school has a three-month summer vacation but not every school has one."

"Other" as an adjective and pronoun:

As an adjective, may be either another in front of singular nouns or other before plurals and uncountables; e.g. "other languages."

May replace singular nouns with another and plural nouns with other; e.g., "One farmer was planting, another was sowing, the others were watching the harvest." The other/s refer to the remaining one/s in a group.

How questions:

May be answered by *by* + noun for questions pertaining to transportation or communication. The noun is a simple form with no article or modifier; e.g., "How did you get here? I got here by car."

May be answered by *by* + ing form for questions about action; e.g.; "How do you speak in front of a group? By practicing."

May be answered by *with* + noun for questions about instrument, equipment, or method used; e.g., "How did you fix the stereo? With a hammer."

May be answered with a single adjective when asking about the description of an object; e.g., "How do you like your coffee? Black." When a complete is used to respond, the adjective is placed at the end of the sentence; e.g.; "I like my coffee black."

How questions about manner require -ly adverbs; e.g., "How do you feed a mountain lion? Carefully."

How question phrases:

How followed by an adjective or a term of quantity, time, manner, distance or frequency; e.g., "How old is Hideo?"

How pharases serve as a unit to act as a question word in an information question pattern; e.g., "How long ago did Sumi leave?" = "When did Sumi leave?"

Answers to how often may be frequency adverbs or time phrases; e.g., "How often do you go to Ginza? Every weekend."

Adverbs of manner:

Usually formed by adding -ly to related adjectives: quick = quickly.

Irregular manner adverbs do not end in -ly and are the same as their adjective equivalents. These include hard, and fast and sometimes slow. *Well* is the adverbial form of the adjective good. As an adjective, *well* refers to a person's health.

They are never placed between a verb and its object; e.g., "I hit the ball hard."

Questions with "what, which, whose":

Often followed by nouns to form questions similar to *how* questions; e.g. "What time did Sumi leave?"

What kind of is used to question sort, style, make, type, color, flavor, and size. *Of* is not used to answer questions of color, flavor or size; e.g., "What color car do you have?"

Causative constructions:

Sentence patter with two verbs which explain how one person causes another person to do something.

Used with the causative verbs *have, make and get.*

Have suggests the person acted upon or is in the employ of the actor; "Jan had the mechanic check her brakes."

Make suggests use of some kind of force or coercion; e.g., "Teachers sometimes make bad students do more homework."

Get usually suggests persuasion; e.g., "I got my best friend to lend me ten dollars."

The causative verb is inflected (i.e., changed). The action verb is in simple form with make or have; e.g., "The mailman made me go to the post office for my package." "While I was there, I had the clerk check the regulations."

The action verb is an infinitive form with *get*; e.g., "Danny got his mother to clean his room every day."

Let and *help* function like causatives. *Let* is like *have* and *make.* *Help* may be formed with an infinitive when the actor is a modifying clause; e.g., "The driver helped the students who came late to find the classroom."

"Get used to" and "be used to":

Idioms that deal with becoming or being accustomed to a situation; e.g., "Diane is getting used to a small apartment." "Takeshi still isn't used to American accents but he understands more now than he used to."

Not to be confused with *used to* + simple verb which suggests a past habit; e.g. "He used to smoke."

Appositives:

Construction in which two words or phrases are next to each and identify the same object or person, with the second usually modifying the first; e.g., "Mr. Takeda, the new dean, seems to be a fine man."

By (a time period):
    Used to refer to an activity which requires an indefinite but considerable length of time before completion. Comple-tion may take place at or before the time mentioned; e.g., "Maybe I'll speak fluent Japanese by the turn of the century--the 22nd!"

Present perfect tense:
    Made from present form of auxiliary *have* and the past participle of a verb. All but about fifty verbs have regular past participle forms ending in -en.
    Auxiliary *have* is identical to the verb *have* except that the auxiliary joins with pronouns and contracts more readily than the verb; "He's gotten all A's this year." Negative contractions are *haven't, hasn't, hadn't.*
    Used to indicate an action or state which was repeated in the past and which may be repeated in the future (e.g., "I have eaten sushi."); an action or state completed at some unspecified past time (usually includes just, already, recently and, if negative, yet: "I haven't seen Sapporo yet"); or an action or state which began some time in the past and has continued to the moment of speaking (usually includes *for* or *since* ("Bill's studied 'kendo' since 1978").

"Just, recently, already, yet":
    Often occur between the auxiliary and main verb, like frequency adverbs. *Just* must occur here (e.g., "Kimi has just seen an old friend"), the others may occur at the end of a sentence; "She's talked to her already."
    Yet is used only in questions and negative statements and always occurs at the end of a sentence; e.g., "She hasn't told her about school yet."
    Just means immediately before speak-ing. *Recently* means a short while ago. *Already* suggests an action sooner than was expected (e.g., "He knows "katakana" already"). *Yet* suggests a time later than expected (e.g., "But he hasn't learned the subway system yet").

Continuous present perfect tense:
    Phrases are made of a present form of auxiliary *have* + *been* + ing form.

Time expressions using *for* or *since* or expressions of recent time (e.g., this week, today) are required; "Michiko has been reading "War and Peace" since 1965."

Emphasizes duration and implies that the action will continue.

Simple past perfect tense:

A verb phrase consisting of auxiliary *have* + a past participle.

Used to express time between two events in the past; e.g., "Sam had talked to Sony on the phone many times before he interviewed with them."

Used to report statements in the simple past or present perfect (reported speech); e.g., "Rita said that she had lost her wallet."

Used to express wishes or unreal conditions about the past; e.g., "She wishes that she hadn't gone." Continuous past perfect tense:

A verb phrase consisting of auxiliary *had* + *been* + ing form.

Used to express duration of a past event that was interrupted or concluded by anothe event; e.g., "Greg had been waiting for an hour when the train finally arrived."

Simple past perfect may be used with little difference in meaning; e.g., "Greg had waited..."

Indirect objects:

Usually a person to whom or for whom something is done.

May be preceded by *to, for, or neither.*

Position in sentence varies according to whether it is introduced by a proposition and the nature of the direct object. If no preposition, the indirect object precedes the direct object; e.g., "Carol asked the student her name." If used with *to* or *for*, the indirect object follows the direct object; e.g., "The student told her name to Carol." If the direct object is a clause, the indirect object precedes it; e.g., "Carol told the girl that she was glad to meet her."

"Say, tell, talk, speak":

Say used usually to introduce a direct or indirect quotation; e.g., "Masao said, "I want to learn English well."

Tell usually requires an indirect object and is rarely used for direct quotations; e.g. "Janice told Ed how to get to the store."

Talk usually refers to a conversation. There is no direct object but it sometimes has an indirect object after to; e.g., "Students can't talk during a test."

Speak can mean to speak when it is followed by to and an indirect object; e.g., "A good teacher always speaks to her students when she sees them outside of class." An alternative meaning is to address in a formal fashion; e.g., "Dan spoke at the commencement."

Noun clauses:

Most often introduced by connective that with *say* or *tell*. Frequently omitted in spoken form; "George said [that] he was sorry to be late."

Ask is used to place a question and never is followed by a that clause. It may have a clause object introduced by *if*; e.g., "The students asked if that meant there would be no test today."

Simple future perfect tense:

Made from *will + have +* past participle.

Used to relate the completion of an act or condition before another action or time in the future.

Must include a future time expression, usually when clauses or phrases introduced by in, next or by; e.g., "By Thursday, the doctor will have treated forty patients."

Continuous future perfect tense:

Made from *will + have +* been + ing form.

Emphasizes the duration of a future event or present situation which reaches into the future. Two time expressions are required, one as a specific time or event and the other as the duration: e.g., "When Hiromi goes to America, she will have been studying English for twelve years."

Simple future perfect tense frequently used instead; e.g., "When Hiromi goes to America, she will have studied English for twelve years."

Transitive/intransitive verbs:

Transitive verbs may take direct objects; intransitive can not.

Some transitive two-word verbs do not allow objects to occur between the words of the verb. They are inseperable; e.g., "Michiko called on her grandmother today."

Separable two-word verbs permit the object between or sometimes require the object between the words. Short noun objects (including pronouns) may occur between the parts of a two-word verb or after the verb; e.g., "He called his friend up." = "He called him up." = "He called up his friend."

Right sometimes modifies two-word verbs to indicate an immediate action; "Each morning at 6, Tom wakes right up."

Tag questions:

Short yes-no questions added to statements.

Used to keep conversation continuation or for confirmation of statement; e.g., "You didn't really leave, did you?"

When the statement is affirmative, the question is negative; e.g., "You told him, didn't you?" When the statement is negative, the question is affirmative; e.g., "You didn't tell him, did you?"

The verb in the question is the first auxiliary of the verb phrase; e.g., "Bob hasn't seen Sam, has he?" If the verb in the statement is a single form of any verb except be, the verb in the question is that same form of do; e.g., "You told him didn't you?" This is also true when the verb is used to or have to; e.g., "Sally had to stay late, didn't she?"

The second word of the tag question must be the subject form of a personal pronoun (e.g., he, she, etc.) or expletives it or there; e.g., "Learning Japanese is hard, isn't it?"

Modal auxiliaries (modals):

Unlike other auxiliaries (do, be, have), modals have no -s form, -ing form or participles.

Comprised of *can/could, will/would, shall/should/ought, may/might, and most.*

Form of the modal does not necessarily indicate the time reference of the sentence. For example, the "past" form (e.g., could) can express the same meaning as *can*. Also, negated modals (e.g., couldn't) don't always mean the opposite of affirmative ones.

Rules are somewhat imprecise. Memori-zation of usage is advised.

Can suggests ability, possibility, opportunity or permission in present ability; e.g., "Elliot can dance like John Travolta."

Could suggests past ability with possibly a changed condition; e.g., "Until yesterday, Jill could ride free with her pass." Also suggests present or future impossibility; "Jim could go to the beach if he didn't have class."

Can or *could* suggest future possibili-ty; e.g., "The doctor can see you at 2 p.m."

Could have + past participle suggests past opportunity not realized; e.g., "The driver could have stopped before the patch of ice." [Implication: he didn't.] Past opportunity realized cannot be expressed with a modal.

Couldn't have + past participle infers past impossibility; e.g., "I'm sorry he couldn't have seen you yesterday."

Present or future permission is expressed with *can* or *may*; e.g., "You may leave now," "You can leave at 3 p.m."

Could or *might* indicates past permission with suggestion of changed condition; e.g., "Before the new govern-ment, no one could vote in Antigua." *Might* is an older form; *could* is more widely used.

Will is used for a future plan, promise or agreement; e.g., "I will finish my homework by 7 so we can go out."

Will + *be* + ing form suggests a continuing future activity; "The prime minister will be meeting with his cabinet tomorrow."

Will + *have* + past participle suggests completion of a future activity; e.g.; "Jessie will have driven 1000 miles by sunset."

Will and *would* are used to make a polite request for future action; e.g., "Will/would you fix me a cup of tea?" Would may be somewhat more polite.

Would is used for present and past contrary-to-fact statements; "If Jack hadn't hurt himself, he'd be captain of the team by now." Note contracted form of would.

Shall/should/ought express advisabili-ty, obligation, expectation and chance.

Shall or *should* are used in affirmative questions of advisability; e.g., "Shall we go to the beach?"

Should may be used for negative questions of advisability (e.g., "Shouldn't we be doing our homework?" [Implication: we aren't.]) or chance happenings; e.g., "If you should go by the store, could you get me a chicken?"

Should or *ought* are used for statements of advisability (e.g., "You ought to careful with appliances"), for unfulfilled obligations (e.g., "I should be studying but 'Cops 'n Bloopers' is on." Fulfilled obligations can not be expressed with a modal) and expectation or likelihood (e.g., "The guests should be arriving soon.")

May is used for present or future permission; e.g., "You may leave now" "You may leave at 2." Past permission can not be expressed with a modal.

May or *might* is used for present or future situations of conjecture (e.g., "He may be at the park.").

May or *might* + be + ing form is used for conjecture about a present activity; e.g., "Ed might be watching TV."

Conjecture about the past is done with *may/might* + *have* + past participle; e.g., "I might have left my notebook on the subway."

Must suggests necessity (e.g., "I must go."), abstention (e.g., "We must not be quick to judge.") or deduction.

Lack of necessity (past and present) is not expressed with a modal because *must* has no past form. *Have to* is used instead; e.g., "Bill doesn't have to leave the country for his visa."

Deduction about a present situation is done using must + simple verb or must + be + ing form; "Our mailman must work hard. He must be delivering a thousand letters today." Deduction about the future requires *must + be + going to*; e.g., "That girl must be going to go to a dance." Deduction about the past requires *must + have + been*; e.g., "Japan must have been dangerous in the samurai era."

All modals (except ought) are followed by simple verbs. Ought is followed by an infinitive; e.g., "You really ought to dress better, Sam."

Adding *not* after the modal the modal makes a negative.

Like all auxiliaries, questions are made by placing the modal before the subject; e.g., "Should we go now?"

Related idioms with modal components may have unrelated meanings; e.g., can't help, would like, would rather (used with than), had better, maybe, willing.

Reported speech:

When a sentence relates an indirect quote from the past without literal restating; e.g., "Jack said that he was jumpy from all the coffee." (Direct quote would be, "Jack said, 'I'm jumpy from all the coffee.'")

Reported speech requires the changing of modals from direct to indirect quotation.

Can becomes *could* ("The boy said he could jump over"), *will* = *would* ("He said he would jump the hedge"), *shall* = *should* ("He asked if he should do it"), *may* = *might* ("I said he might if he was careful"), *must* = *had to* ("He replied that sometimes a boy just had to do what a boy had to do."

Should and *ought* do not change in reported speech; e.g., "Larry said, "I ought to try it myself." = "He said he ought to try it himself."

Imperatives:

Sentence type usually used for giving instructions or making requests (usually with please at beginning or end of the sentence).

Imperatives have no expressed subject and begin with the verb phrase; e.g., "Get off the bus at Main Street."

Negative forms may be made as usual or with *never* in the beginning position or with *ever* and a negative verb; e.g., "Don't ever eat ice cream too fast." = "Never eat ice cream too fast."

Subjunctives:

These are usually phrases of suggestion introduced by a verb phrase beginning with *that*; e.g., "Danielle suggested that Bob go to Yale."

Usually, the tenses of different verbs in the same sentence agree; e.g. "I know that you agree." There is no agreement of tense sequence in subjunctive objects because the verb in the clause (after that) does not exist at the time of speaking; "She has often urged that he go someplace prestigious."

Verbs taking subjunctive noun-clause objects include: advise, ask, demand, forbid, insist, prefer, propose, recommend, request, require, suggest, urge among others.

Noun-clause objects:

When a clause functions as a direct object, the word order is altered so the verb follows the subject: "Where is my book?" = "Do you know where my book is?"

Auxiliaries usually precede the subject. In noun clauses, though, they follow the subject; e.g., "Why is she laughing?" = "Do you know why she is laughing?"

Auxiliary *do* vanishes when changed to a noun clause but the inflection (ending) it had is transfered to the main verb of the noun clause; e.g.; "Where does Bob go on weekends?" = "I wonder where Bob goes on weekends."

Infinitive phrases:

Usually a statement, not a question, followed by an s-form verb; e.g., "To learn a foreign language is valuable."

The infinitive phrase as subject may appear at the end of a sentence if the sentence begins with the anticipatory *it*; e.g., "It is very difficult for me to learn one." = "To learn one is very difficult for me."

Subjects of infinitives appear before the infinitive; e.g., "Teachers expect students to study." (The phrase "students to study" is the direct object of "teaches expect.")

In compound sentences, the infinitive is frequently abbreviated to *to* if the phrases' verbs are the same; "Many young Americans want to visit Japan but many older ones don't want to."

Infinitives may modify nouns (e.g., "Noriko has a letter to write"), adjectives or adverbs (e.g., "Don't be afraid to fail"), verbs (e.g., "Don't hesitate to ask") and compound indefinites (someone, anyone, anything, etc.); e.g., "There isn't anything to eat in my house."

Object phrases beginning with question words (which, why, how, etc.) often take infinitives; e.g., "I can't decide how to teach infinitives." ("how to teach infinitives" is the object of "decide.")

Imperatives in direct quotes become infinitives in reported speech; e.g., "Phyllis said, "Eat a lot, Bill." = "Phyllis told Bill to eat a lot."

Marked and unmarked adjective clauses:

Each adjective clause has a subject and a verb and modifies the word preceding them; e.g., "Students who study the hardest succeed the fastest." In this example, the clause marker also serves as clause subject.

Most adjective clauses require clause markers to indicate their beginning; e.g. "I like books that challenge my mind." However, unmarked clauses have no clause markers (or may take an optional which or that), making the clauses difficult to recognize; e.g. "They fill me with thoughts [that] I never had."

The above adjective clauses are essential for the meaning of their sentences. For this reason, they are called "restrictive adjective clauses." "Non-restrictive adjective clauses" are freqent-ly set off by commas, are non-essential and may be deleted without affecting the sentence's meaning; e.g., "Grammar, which can get awfully boring, really is essential."

Gerunds:

-Ing forms which serve as subjects.

Usually function as uncountables although sometimes a plural ending may be added; e.g., readings, writings, teachings.

Verbal in nature since it can take its own subject and object; e.g., "My failing to explain this material well could cause some confusion."

Some verbs often take gerunds as objects but won't take infinitives; e.g., "Jack considers watching TV challenging." Other verbs will take either a gerund or an infinitive as objects; e.g., "He prefers concentrating [or to concentrate] on it alone."

Sense perception verbs (notice, hear, observe, smell, see, feel, watch) may take simple or gerund objects but not infinitives; e.g., "She heard singing in the other room."

-Ing form objects emphasize on-going action. Simple verbs suggest that the action is finished; e.g., "She heard someone sing in the other room." [Implication: she's not singing now.]

Forget and *remember* may take either a gerund or infinitive object with different meanings. Gerund objects express actions occuring before the main verb; e.g., "Hideo remembers telling Pete he would be absent." Infinitive objects with remember express action after the main verb; e.g., "Please remember to put out the candle." With *forget*, infinitive objects express actions which won't or shouldn't occur; e.g., "Don't forget to extinguish it."

-Ing forms as noun modifiers:

Also called present participles or verbal adjectives.

Appear before nouns to be modified (e.g., "blinding light," "intriguing premise"), after a noun to be modified (e.g., "I find my clothes boring.") or after the verb be (e.g., "Driving is frustrating.")

-Ing forms in time and after prepositions:

Must be used after time words *before, after, until, since while* and *when*;e.g., "Tomiko shrieked before dropping the dish." Infinitives may never follow these time words.

Must be used immediately after all prepositions except *to*; e.g., "Dick planned on going to Bangkok over the holidays."

Passive voice:

Unlike the usual "active voice," passive voice puts the performer of the action at the end of the sentence or may delete it altogether, putting the object of the action at the beginning; e.g., "The dish was dropped by Tomiko."

Only transitive verbs may be used with the passive voice.

Passive sentences always contain auxiliary *be* and a past participle. Other auxiliaries may precede *be*; e.g., "Homework must be completed (by all students)."

Used when the specific performer of the action is unknown (e.g., "Judy's car was made in Japan"), when we choose not to mention the performer (e.g., "Beth was told she would have to repeat the course"), when we want to emphasize the object (e.g., "Passports are checked carefully," "Electricity was discovered by Ben Franklin."

With *have* in causative constructions, the performer is frequently omitted because it is not important. These constructions are not true passives because they don't contain be but they are very similar; e.g., "The IRS has tax returns sent to local centers." (What could be less important than a taxpayer?)

Past participles used as noun modifiers also are related to passives; "Trucking is a regulated industry." [We don't know who regulates.]

Comparisons:

Complete sameness may be expressed with *the same as* (e.g., "Hideo's Toyota is the same as Susan's.") or with *alike*; e.g., "Hideo's and Susan's Toyotas are alike."

Similarity in many respects is indicated with *like*; e.g., "Phil's teaching style is like Jack's: 'laid back.'"

Similarity in one respect is shown with *the same* + noun (e.g., "Edgar and Jackie are the same age") or with *the same* + noun + *as*; e.g., "Edgar is the same age as Jackie (is)") or *with as* + adj/adv/(many + noun) + *as*; e.g., "George's watercolor was as lovely as Sachiko's." "I didn't do as many paintings as they did."

Almost, nearly, and *about* limit similarity; e.g., "Hideo's Toyota is almost the same as Susan's." *Just* and *exactly* enhance the similarity; "Phil's teaching style is just like Jack's."

Statements of difference are formed with *differs* from (e.g., "Jan's dog differs from Al's in color"), or different from; e.g., "They're both different from Jack's."

Somewhat and *a little* limit the difference; e.g., "Jan's dog is somewhat browner than Al's." *Quite, very* and *entirely* enhance the difference; e.g., "Their both entirely different from Jack's."

Comparison of two different groups:

If the comparative adjective or adverb ends in -er, it will usually be followed by *than*.

One-syllable adjectives and adverbs are made into comparative by merely adding -er to the end; e.g., faster. If they end in -y, the ending is -ier; e.g., happier.

Similarity in one respect is shown with *the same* + noun (e.g., "Edgar and Jackie are the same age"), or with *the same* + noun + *as*; e.g., "Edgar is the same age as Jackie."

If adjectives or adverbs have more than two syllables, they usually don't have comparatives. Instead, they take *more* before and *than* after; e.g., "more beautiful than." May also be used with less instead of more.

Double comparatives are used to express degree to which one characteristic is dependent on another; e.g., "The faster I run, the 'behinder' I get."

Superlatives:

Used to indicate the highest degree of the adjective or adverb in a group of three or more; "She was the fairest of them all."

One syllable superlatives end in -est. Adjectives or adverbs ending in -y have superlatives ending in -iest. Most adjectives or adverbs with more than two syllables do not have superlatives. Instead, they use *the most*; "She was the most beautiful at the ball." *Least* is used as the opposite of most.

Irregular comparative and superlative forms: good, better, best; well, better, best; bad, worse, worst; badly, worse, worst; little, less, least; much, more, most; many, more, most; far, farther, farthest.

Conditional "if" clauses:

Express conditions which may produce the imagined result described in the main clause.

Future conditions are indicated in the present tense; e.g., "She'll get a good grade if she studies."

Present conditions are indicated in the past tense. Result phrase includes one of the modals *would, could*, or *might*; e.g., "If Jack ate better, he might lose weight."

Past conditions are indicated in the past perfect tense (*had* + past participle) with result clause including *would, could*, or *might* and the present perfect tense (*have* + past participle); e.g., "I would have come sooner if I'd known you were sick."

"Unless" conditional clauses:

Have the same form as if clauses but negatives are affirmative and affirmatives are negative; e.g., "Jack might not lose weight unless he eats better."

May follow or precede the result clause; e.g. "Unless he eats better, Jack might not lose weight."

"Whether or not" clauses:

Indicate that there is no causal relationship between the clauses. May be considered the opposite of *if* clauses.

Very similar to *if* clauses in structure except that *or not* usually appears at the end of the conditional clause; e.g., "Emma's going to the mountains whether Haruko goes or not." *Or not* may occur with *whether* if the conditional clause is especially long and possibly confusing; e.g., "She's driving whether or not Haruko decides to help pay for the gas."

Whether may also suggest alternatives in object clauses (e.g., "Did Sue say whether she was meeting Paul or Ted tomorrow?) or in infinitive phrases; e.g., "She doesn't know whether to go out or stay home?"

Use of "hope":

When expressing hope for an unknown something related to self, an infinitive or *that* clause may be used with the same meaning; e.g., "I hope to go to Kyoto soon." = "I hope (that) I can go to Kyoto soon."

Only a *that* clause can be used to express hope relating to another person; e.g., "Sally hopes (that) her students are having a good Christmas."

Only a present tense may be used to express hope about the unknown present; e.g., "She hopes (that) they don't forget their English over the holidays."

Only a past tense may be used to express hope in the unknown past; e.g., "She hopes (that) they didn't eat too much on New Year's Day."

Result and reason:

In complex sentences, an independent clause often tells the result of a dependent clause which gives the reason for it.

Reasons are introduced by clause markers which indicate this relationship: *because, as,* and *since* (not time); e.g., "I went to the gym since my class was cancelled."

This order may be reversed, presenting the reason first. This construction emphasizes the reason over the result and may be considered somewhat more formal; e.g., "Because Sarah was among the first to arrive, she decided to tour the house." A pronoun is usually used in the second clause since the noun referant is in the first clause.

Also formal is the use of *thus, therefore, hence, consequently* and *as a result* which do not connect clauses but are used to begin a second sentence; e.g., "Sarah was among the first to arrive. As a result, she decided to tour the house." A semicolon with *and* may be used to join the sentences.

Because of also is used to express reason; e.g., "Dan wanted to go hiking because of the beautiful weather."

To present informally the same reason and result relationship as the formal *thus, hence,* etc., *so* is commonly used; e.g., "Sarah arrived early so she practiced reading katakana on the billboards."

So + adj/adv + *that* tells the result of an action caused by the degree of a characteristic; "Jerry's so ambitious (that) he never has time for friends." Don't confuse this with *so that* which is used to indicate purpose and contains a modal such as *can, could, will,* or *would*; e.g., "Jerry is ambitious so (that) he can succeed." [That is frequently omitted in both constructions.]

Purpose is also told by an infinitive and the optional *in order* (e.g., "Jerry works hard (in order) to succeed") or by *for* + noun; e.g, "He's striving for financial independence."

Such/so + (modifier + noun) + *that* is a pattern which, like *so* + adj/adv + *that*, also gives the result and degree relationship; e.g., "Japan is such a fascinating country that I would like to stay several years."

The reason + *why/that* + *is that* emphasizes the reason over the result; "Hiroshi said the reason (that) he didn't have his assignment was that he had been robbed by pirates."

What at the beginning of a question with *for* at the end means why; "What did the pirates take his homework for?" Because this is a colloquial expression, it defies grammatical explanation and allows ending a construction with a preposition.

Concession statements:

Used with clauses to indicate unexpected results.

The dependent clause is introduced by *although* and *even though* and may precede or follow the result clause; e.g., "Even though speaking English is easy for native speakers, foreigners find it very difficult." = "Foreigners find speaking English difficult even though it's easy for native speakers."

In spite of may be followed by a noun, an -ing form or a clause introduced by *the fact that*; "In spite of the fact that Janice was late, we got to the show on time."

But at the beginning of a result clause and *anyway* at the end suggests the reason clause is insignificant; e.g., "The day was cloudy but we had fun at the park anyway."

Besides and *other than* are used to contrast a solitary option; "Jun didn't want to visit anyplace besides L.A."

To contrast a statement just made, *however* is used to relate (but not actually join) sentences; e.g., "Congratulations! You've just completed your grammar review. However, now you have to be able to explain the stuff to your students!"

APPENDIX: PRIVATE ENGLISH SCHOOLS

The following private English schools in Japan all employ native speakers as English instructors and usually are in need of such teachers. The list is alphabetical and contains schools listed earlier in the second edition of <u>JOBS IN JAPAN</u> (indicated by "(JIJ)" in the listing), schools believed to have opened within the last three years (designated as "(new)" in the listing) and others. Mention in this directory is no assurance of quality. It's advisable to ask current employees (especially foreign teachers) about conditions at the school before making any type of commitment.

TOKYO AREA ("03" telephone prefix)

* ABC; Tokyo, Chuo-ku, Nihonbashi, Murofuji Goe Bldg.; (new); Tel. 242-7261.
* Academia; Tokyo, Shibuya-ku, Tomigaya 1-35; (new); Tel. 465-8939.
* Access, Teisen Kandabashi Bldg. 5F, 1-27 Nishiki, Kanda, Tokyo; Tel. 291-6751.
* Albion Gakuin; 167, Tokyo, Suginami-ku, Showan 3-26-24; Tel. 333-9081. Four foreign teachers. (JIJ).
* Alec Gaigo Gakuin; 150, Tokyo, Shibuya 1-14-13 Daini Kobayashi Bldg. 5F; Tel. 400-4515. Nine foreign teachers. (JIJ).
* Alf English School; Tokyo, Adachi-ku, Nishi Arai 2-18; (new); Tel. 896-0460.
* Alfa English School; Tokyo, Shibuya, Komatsu Bldg.; (new); Tel. 486-8185.
* Alfa English School; Tokyo, Shibuya, Aoyama Laurel Bldg.; (new); Tel. 498-2462.
* Alpha English School, 4-7 Shimo Ishigami, Tokyo; Tel. 904-3424.
* American Academy; Tokyo, Shinagawa-ku, Nishi Gotanda 2-24; (new); Tel. 495-0881.
* American Family Club; Tokyo, Shibuya-ku, Minami Hiradai 12; (new); Tel. 476-2241.
* American House Eikaiwa Center; 188, Tokyo, Tanashi-shi, Hommachi 5-4-1; Tel. 0424-64-0930. Three foreign teachers. (JIJ).

* American Radio; Tokyo, Chiyoda-ku, Misaki, Misaki-cho, Florence Bldg.; (new); Tel. 265-5705.

* Anglo World; Tokyo; (new); Tel. 648-6881.

* Anglo-Continental Educational Group, 3-15 Roppongi, Minato-ku, Tokyo; Tel. 582-9735.

* Ann's American Conversation Kyoshitsu, 2-19 Takadanobaba, Shinjuku-ku, Tokyo; Tel. 205-2425.

* Aoki Shigeru; Tokyo, Adachi-ku, Adachi 4-30; (new); Tel. 887-0768.

* Aoyama English School; Tokyo, Minato-ku, Minami-Aoyama 2-2; (new); Tel. 405-5563.

* ASA; 160, Tokyo, Shinjuku-ku, Nishi-Shinjuku 1-19-6, Yamate Shinjukku Bldg.; Tel. 348-3333. 150 foreign teachers, selective hiring. (JIJ).

* Asahi Culture Center; 160, Tokyo, Nishi-Shinjuku, 2-6-1 1, Sumitomo Bldg.; Tel. 344-1941. Unlikely to sponsor but employs 22 foreign teachers. (JIJ).

* Asia Center/PARC; 101, Tokyo, Chiyoda-ku, Kanda, Jimbocho 1-30, Seiko Bldg. 4F; Tel. 291-5901. All foreign teachers (3). (JIJ).

* Athenee Francais; 101, Tokyo, Chiyoda-ku, Kanda, 2-11 Surugadai; Tel. 291-3391. Teaches many languages. 25 foreign teachers. (JIJ).

* Azabu Academy; 106, Tokyo, Roppongi 3-14-12, Shuwa Roppongi Bldg. #701; Tel. 404-2841. Accelerated courses. All foreign teachers (8). (JIJ).

* Baberu Honyaku Gakuin, NS Bldg. 2-2-3 Sarugaku-cho, Chiyoda-ku, Tokyo 101; Tel. 295-5155. 2 foreign teachers. (JIJ).

* Barcino School; Tokyo, Shibuya-ku, Dogenzaka 1-15; (new); Tel. 496-5955.

* BEC; 160, Tokyo, Shinjuku 3-28-10; Tel. 352-2958. Large school with 73 foreign teachers. (JIJ).

* Berkeley House Center, Topure Bldg. 4-2, Gobancho, Chiyoda-ku, Tokyo 102; Tel. 262-2711. TESL background, North American only. (JIJ).

* Berlitz School, Asia Bldg., Kami Minami, Shibuya-ku, Tokyo; Tel. 461-5201.

* Berlitz School, Daini Koa Bldg. 1-11-39 Akasaka, Minato-ku, Tokyo 107; Tel. 584-4211. World-wide chain. 190 foreign teachers. (JIJ).

* Berlitz; Tokyo, Chuo-ku, Nihonbashi, Sanken Muromachi Bldg.; (new); Tel. 243-0381.

* Berlitz; Tokyo, Chuo-ku, Nihonbashi, Dick Bldg.; (new); Tel. 274-6701.

* Berlitz; Tokyo, Meguro-ku, Jiyugaoka, Obara Bldg.; (new); Tel. 724-3781.

* Berlitz; Tokyo, Minato-ku, Kita Aoyama 3-3; (new); Tel. 423-0361.

* Berlitz; Tokyo, Nishi Shinjuku, Daini Takakura Bldg.; (new); Tel. 342-4751.

* Berlitz; Tokyo, Toyoshima-ku, Higashi Ikebukuro, Soba Bldg.; (new); Tel. 983-6221.

* Best; Tokyo, Yotsuya 3-chome, Fudosan Kaikan 503; (new); Tel. 351-4191.

* Bilingual Tokyo; 150, Tokyo, Shibuya-ku, Utagawa-cho 39-2, Village 80 Bldg. 4F; Tel. 477-1858. Large school with 170 foreign teachers. (JIJ).

* Bougnan English School; Toyoshima-ku, Higashi Ikebukuro 1-25-3; (new); Tel. 983-7151.

* Bravis School of Languages, Taisei Bldg., 1-1-18 Akasaka, Tokyo; Tel. 586-1828.

* Bridge Center; Tokyo, Chuo-ku, Kyobashi, Irifune Honkan Bldg.; (new); Tel. 281-4066.

* Brittania Gaigo Gakuin; 120, Tokyo, Adachi-ku, Ayase 3-3-1, Hoshi Bldg. 3F; Tel. 629-8681. All British teachers (18). (JIJ).

* Bunka Language Center; Tokyo, Shibuya-ku, Yoyogi 3-22; (new); Tel. 370-3111.

* Bunsai Kenkyujo; Tokyo, Shinjuku-ku, Takadanobaba, Chiyoda Seimei Bldg.; (new); Tel. 209-4971.

* Business Heights English Conversation School, 5-67 Nakano, Nakano-ku, Tokyo; Tel. 388-3227.

* BUV; Tokyo, Suginami-ku, Shimo Ibusan, Nakae Bldg.; (new); Tel. 397-5609.

* Buzz International; Tokyo, Minato-ku, Roppongi 7-18; (new); Tel. 402-9863.

* Cambridge Academy; Tokyo, Shibuya-ku, Udogawa 2; (new); Tel. 462-2613.

* Cambridge English School; 160, Tokyo, Nishi-Shinjuku 1-13-12, Showa Bldg.; Tel. 348-0181. Teachers must have RSA credential (British). (JIJ).

* CCC, 1-15 Jingumae, Shibuya-ku, Tokyo; Tel. 404-6888.

* Century Eigo Gakuin; 105, Tokyo, Minato-ku, Hammamatsu-cho 1-25-3; Tel. 434-9484. 6 foreign teachers. (JIJ).

* Century Language School; Tokyo, Minato-ku, Hamamatsu Watanabe Bldg.; (new); Tel. 434-7484.

* Children Eigo Gakuin, 1-23 Toshima, Kita-ku, Tokyo; Tel. 912-8526.

* Children English School; Tokyo, Nerima-ku, Fujimidai 2-4; (new); Tel. 990-0664.

* Chuo Eigo Gakuin, 2-23 Nakano, Nakano-ku, Tokyo; Tel. 382-2098.

* Chuo Steno College; 160, Tokyo, Nishi-Shinjuku 7-4-7, Ota Bldg.; Tel. 362-4191. 4 foreign teachers. (JIJ).

* CIC; Tokyo, Minato-ku, Kita Aoyama 3-5; (new); Tel. 475-0261.

* CLC; 103, Tokyo, Chuo-ku, Yaesu 1-9-13, Yaesu Ekimae Godo Bldg. 5F; Tel. 275-0151. All foreign teachers (20). (JIJ).

* Clover English Center; Tokyo, Kita-ku, Akabane, Sanyo Bldg.; (new); Tel. 903-3611.

* Comet Eikaiwa School, Sakata Bldg. 2F, 1-16-14 Hyakunin-cho, Shinjuku-ku, Tokyo; Tel. 362-3909.

* Comet International; Tokyo, Shinagawa-ku, Kamiozaki 4-5; (new); Tel. 494-7166.

* Conan Gaigo School; 102, Tokyo, Chiyoda-ku, Ichiban-cho 4, Sagamiya Bldg.; Tel. 234-3358. 6 foreign teachers. (JIJ).

* Conan Language School; Tokyo, Shibuya-ku, Engaku Miura Bldg.; (new); Tel. 463-9712.

* The Concord School of English, Kuroda Heights, 6-6-16 Akasaka, Minato-ku, Tokyo; Tel. 585-1084.

* Cosmo Language Center; Tokyo, Minato-ku, Akasaka, Kaneharu Bldg.; (new); Tel. 582-0561.

* Cosmopolitan Language Institute, Yaesu B Bldg., Yaesu 1-8-9, Chuo-ku, Tokyo 103 Tel. 273-7878. Classes from 8 a.m. to 9 p.m. Principly for businessmen.

* Cosmopolitan; Tokyo, Toyoshima-ku, Nishi Ikebukuro 1-29; (new); Tel. 988-8317.

* Create English School; Tokyo, Shinjuku 4-2; (new); Tel. 354-4601.

* Cross Continental, SK Bldg., Miyamasuzaka 14-8, Shibuya-ku, Tokyo 150 Tel. 409-0051.

* Deck's International School, Fujio Bldg. 2F & 3F, 3-49-3 Chuo, Nakano-ku, Tokyo; Tel. 367-5032.
* Don Bosco English Conversation Club, 3-11 Arakawa, Tokyo; Tel. 801-8296.
* East West English Center, Sanno Grand Bldg., Nagatacho, Chiyoda-ku, Tokyo; Tel. 581-7571.
* ECC; 160, Tokyo, Shinjuku-ku, Kabuki-cho 1-5-4, Dairoku Arai Bldg.; Tel. 209-3733. Very large chain. 44 schools and 200 foreign teachers. (JIJ).
* ECC; Tokyo, Chiyoda-ku, Uchikanda, Daini Tomoe Bldg.; (new); Tel. 256-1703.
* ECC; Tokyo, Nishi Ikebukuro, Chitoku Bldg.; (new); Tel. 989-0531.
* ECS, Sogo Dairoku Bldg., 12-4 Hirakawa-cho 1-chome, Chiyoda-ku, Tokyo; Tel. 230-3286.
* Edward English Conversation School, 3-38 Soshigaya, Setagaya-ku, Tokyo; Tel.482-2250.
* Eifel School; Shinjuku-ku, Shimoochiai, Nihon Tsuyaku Kyokai Bldg.; (new); Tel. 367-0615.
* Eigo Gakuin; 164, Tokyo, Nakano-ku, Nakano 2-23-1; Tel. 380-6970. 2 foreign teachers. (JIJ).
* Eigo Semmon Kenkyujo; 110, Tokyo, Higashi Ueno 6-2-2, Maruyoshi Bldg.; Tel. 844-3104. 2 foreign teachers. (JIJ).
* Eikaiwa Gakuin; 185, Kunitachi-shi, Higashi 1-6, Hoshino Bldg.; Tel. 0425-72-3719. All American teachers (13). (JIJ).
* ELA, 2-20 Kamiosaki, Shinagawa-ku, Tokyo; Tel. 491-4460.
* ELC; Tokyo, Toyoshima-ku, Sugamo 3-33; (new); Tel. 910-6680.
* ELEC; 101, Tokyo, Chiyoda-ku, Kanda, 3-8 Jimbocho; Tel. 265-8911. Large school with all foreign teachers (100). (JIJ).
* ELI; Tokyo, Toyoshima-ku, Higashi Ikebukuro, Osumi Bldg.; (new); Tel. 980-0401.
* English Den, 5-14-7 Hirai Nakagawa, Edogawa-ku Tel. 617-7278.
* English House, 2-23 Nishi Ikebukuro, Tokyo; Tel. 988-1743.
* English House, 5-11 Hon, Nakano-ku, Tokyo; Tel. 383-6454.

* English House; Tokyo, Chiyoda-ku, Kanda, Kamiho, Noguchi Daini Bldg.; (new); Tel. 291-5848.

* English Language Center, Ogawa Bldg., Jinbocho, Kanda, Tokyo; Tel. 295-2356.

* English Private School, 2-24 Ogibashi, Koto-ku, Tokyo; Tel. 645-1314.

* English Salon Jun; Tokyo, Minato-ku, Shin Hashinonaka Bldg.; (new); Tel. 508-0473.

* English Service; 170, Tokyo, Higashi Ikebukuro 3-1-4, Maison Sunshine 1246; Tel. 988-3611. All foreign teachers (10). (JIJ).

* English Telephone Club, 136 Minami Oizumi, Nerima-ku, Tokyo; Tel. 924-3853.

* English Train; Tokyo, Minato-ku, Nishi Azabu 2-7; (new); Tel. 486-9395.

* English Village, 3-10-10 Kamiosaki, Shinagawa-ku, Tokyo 141 Tel. 446-3837.

* ENL; Tokyo, Taito-ku, Moto Asakusa Kaibara Bldg.; (new); Tel. 842-6357.

* Erokens Language School; Tokyo, Minato-ku, Ropponi 7-18; (new); Tel. 405-7565.

* ESC; Tokyo, Setagaya-ku, Kamikitazawa 4-12; (new); Tel. 329-3993.

* Espero Language School; Tokyo, Shibuya-ku, Yoyogi 1-57; (new); Tel. 370-0399.

* Eternity; Tokyo, Shinjuku Rafu Kaikan; (new); Tel. 350-6764.

* Eto Shingaku; Tokyo, Eto, Toyo 5-1; (new); Tel. 645-4033.

* Euro Center Japan, Fukai Bldg., Surugadai, Kanda, Tokyo; Tel. 295-5441.

* Evergreen Eigo Gakuin; 150, Tokyo, Meguro-ku, 1-21-2 Yutenji; Tel. 713-4958. 7 foreign teachers. (JIJ).

* Excellence; 102, Tokyo, Chiyoda-ku, 4 Bancho 6, Palais Blanc 303. Personally recommended by a former teacher as being especially honest. (JIJ).

* Executive Gogaku Center; 107, Tokyo, Akasaka 1-9-20, Koa Dai 16 Bldg.; Tel. 585-6401. Large chain. 20 foreign teachers. Comparatively poor pay. (JIJ).

* Executive School; Tokyo, Chiyoda-ku, Kasumigaseki 3-2; (new); Tel. 581-5631.

* FF Eigo Kyoshitsu, 3-1 Yoyogi, Tokyo; Tel. 375-5261.

* FIA, Fukumaru Bldg., 4-26-12 Minami Koenji, Suginami-ku, Tokyo 166 Tel. 314-6241.

* FIS; 155, Tokyo, Setagaya-ku, Kitazawa 2-10-15; Tel. 468-8598. 13 foreign teachers. (JIJ).

* FJ Associates; Tokyo, Chuo-ku, Hachobori Fuji Bldg.; (new); Tel. 553-5935.

* FL Center; 150, Tokyo, Shibuya-ku, Shibuya 2-19-20, Iwasaki Bldg. 3F; Tel. 400-9811. All foreign teachers (10). Experience required. (JIJ).

* FL Center; Tokyo, Chiyoda-ku, Iidabashi 3-6; (new); Tel. 262-5817.

* Fujimi English Conversation Gakuin, 2-4 Fujimi, Chiyoda-ku, Tokyo; Tel. 264-3957.

* Future Communication Center, Kami Ichi Bldg., Nishi Shinbashi, Minato-ku, Tokyo; Tel. 591-1436.

* Gaikokugo Noryoku Kaihatsu Center, Asahi Bldg., Uchikanda, Tokyo; Tel. 291-2288.

* Gakusei no Ie, 2-23-27 Hyakunin-cho, Shinjuku-ku, Tokyo; Tel. 362-2271.

* Gakusei no Ie; Tokyo, Toyoshima-ku, Mejiro 3-17; (new); Tel. 950-8671.

* GEM; 150, Tokyo, Shibuya-ku, Shibuya 1-13-5, Daikyo Bldg. 4F; Tel. 406-8031. 15 foreign teachers. (JIJ).

* Genzai English School; Tokyo, Shibuya-ku, Yoyogi, Daini Nogi Bldg.; (new); Tel. 370-2059.

* Ginza Beikaiwa Salon; 104, Tokyo, Chuo-ku 5-9-13 Nakamura Bldg.; Tel. 573-7427. All foreign teachers (19). (JIJ).

* Global English Program; Tokyo, Minato-ku, Akasaka 2-16; (new); Tel. 582-1679.

* Gogaku Jishu Kunrenjo, Yamaguchi Bldg., Higashi Ikebukuro, Tokyo; Tel. 982-2208.

* Gohoshi Gakuin; Tokyo, Minato-ku, Akasaka, Suzuki Bldg.; (new); Tel. 582-5551.

* Goken Center; Tokyo, Minato-ku, Akasaka 9-1; (new); Tel. 470-6546.

* Goodwill, 4-8 Takanawa, Minato-ku, Tokyo; Tel. 445-7845.

* Green English School; Tokyo, Shinagawa-ku, Nishi Gotanda 2-24; (new); Tel. 492-2626.

* Greg School; Tokyo, Shibuya-ku, Dogenza-ka, Umehara Bldg.; (new); Tel. 464-7481.

* Gregg/Tokyo Business School; 152, Tokyo, Meguro-ku, 1-14-16 Jugaoka; Tel. 724-0552. One of the largest schools with 102 foreign teachers. (JIJ).

* Gregg Language School; Chiyoda-ku, Kanda, Komakawadai, Segawa Bldg.; (new); Tel. 295-4131.

* Hamamatsu School; Tokyo, Minato-ku, Hamamatsu, Sekai Boeki Bldg.; (new); Tel. 435-5751.

* Hampton/Pan Pacific School of English, Daini Komatsu Bldg. 4F, 2-14-17 Shibuya, Tokyo 150; Tel. 406-1231. Instructors must have TEFL background. British preferred. (JIJ).

* Harajuku Gaigo Gakuin; 151, Tokyo, Shibuya-ku, Jingumae 5-11-8; Tel. 406-4604. 15 foreign teachers. (JIJ).

* Harajuku Language School; Tokyo, Shibuya-ku, Jingumae 5-11; (new); Tel. 400-8695.

* Harold School; Suginami-ku, Koenji Kita 2-3; (new); Tel.338-5511.

* Harrison Language Service; Tokyo, Minato-ku, Roppongi 7-15; (new); Tel. 423-1983.

* Hibiya Gakuin English School, 2-7 Higashi Gotanda, Shinagawa-ku, Tokyo; Tel. 442-9755.

* Hills Saino Kaihatsu Kenkyujo, 3-6 Higashi Yaguchi, Otaku, Tokyo; Tel. 734-2771.

* Honan English Academy; Tokyo, Suginami-ku, Honan 2-23; (new); Tel. 313-1700.

* Horin Academia, FI Bldg. 6F, 1-26-5 Takadanobaba, Shinjuku-ku, Tokyo 160; Tel. 200-7771. Large school with 60 foreign teachers. (JIJ).

* IBS Harajuku, 6-31 Jingumae, Shibuya-ku, Tokyo; Tel. 486-7317.

* IBS; Tokyo, Minato-ku, Roppongi, Kyodo Bldg.; (new); Tel. 404-1684.

* ICA; 171, Tokyo, Toyoshima-ku, Nishi Ikebukuro, 1-16-10; Tel. 984-2476. Related to San Antonio College. (JIJ).

* ICA; Tokyo, Toyoshima-ku, Minamai Otsuka, Yamate Bldg.; (new); Tel. 947-6711.

* ICA; Tokyo, Toyoshima-ku, Nishi Ikebuku-ro, Mikasa Bldg.; (new); Tel. 981-7988.

* ICCS, 1-15 Tabata, Kita-ku, Tokyo; Tel. 823-4394.

* ICE; Tokyo, Minato-ku, Akasaka 3-14; (new); Tel. 584-2800.

* ICE; Tokyo, Minato-ku, Takanawa 4-7; (new); Tel. 440-1800.

* ICF, 1-38 Akazutsumi, Setagaya-ku, Tokyo; Tel. 322-4726.

* IEI; Tokyo, Shinjuku-ku, Shimoochiai, Mejiro, Daiwada Bldg.; (new); Tel. 952-8081.

* IF Gaigo Gakuin; 101, Tokyo, Chiyoda-ku, Kanda, Konya-cho 21-8; Tel. 252-7747. 5 foreign teachers. (JIJ).

* IHS; 171, Tokyo, Toyoshima-ku, Mejiro 2-34-3; Tel. 989-9851. International Hospita-lity Society. 30 foreign teachers. (JIJ).

* Ikeda Jinichi; Tokyo, Koto-ku, Toyo 3-16; (new); Tel. 644-0680.

* IL Eigo Kyoshitsu, 1-49 Nishi Nippori, Arakawa-ku, Tokyo; Tel. 807-6414.

* ILC; 101, Tokyo, Chiyoda-ku, Jinden, Jimbocho 2-1, Iwanami Jimbocho Bldg. 9F; Tel. 954-5173. All foreign teachers (70), mostly British. (JIJ).

* ILS; Tokyo, Bunkyo-ku, Yayoi 2-7; (new); Tel. 816-2503.

* InterEnglish School; Tokyo, Adachi-ku, Umeda 7-5; (new); Tel. 852-1722.

* Interlang School and Service; 107, Tokyo, Kita-Aoyama 2-14-6, Bell Commons 7F; Tel. 497-5451. 15 foreign teachers using Interlang method. (JIJ).

* Interlingua Club; 154, Tokyo, Meguro-ku, Yutenji 2-15-17; Tel. 791-5561. 3 foreign teachers. (JIJ).

* Interlink; Tokyo, Minato-ku, Akasaka, Rokan Bldg.; (new); Tel. 588-0022.

* Int'l Business Lang. Svc., Yanagiya Bldg., 1-16-6 Shinbashi, Minato-ku, Tokyo; Tel. 591-2770.

* Int'l Education Service, Shin Taiso Bldg., 2-10-7 Dogenzaka, Shibuya, Tokyo 150 Tel. 463-5396.

* Int'l Institute of Japan; 150, Tokyo, Jingumae 4-2-11, Belair Garden Bldg. 2F; Tel. 405-0754. 15 foreign teachers. (JIJ).

* InterTokyo; 107 Tokyo, Minato-ku, Akasaka 8-5-32, Yamakatsu Bldg. 7F; Tel. 479-4861. 2 foreign teachers. (JIJ).

* InterWorld; Tokyo, Minato-ku, Mita, Mitoyo Bldg.; (new); Tel. 453-0343.

* InterWorld; Tokyo, Nishi Shinjuku, Hirata Bldg.; (new); Tel. 371-5091.

* IPS; Tokyo, Shibuya-ku, Jingumae 6-31; (new); Tel. 400-7793.

* Ishikawa Gakuin; 124, Tokyo, Katsushika-ku, 3-29-12 Tateishi; Tel. 697-2222. Emphasizes practical English. 7 foreign teachers. (JIJ).

* ISS; 102, Tokyo, Chiyoda-ku, Kojimachi, 1-6 Sogo Daisan Bldg. Bekkan 5F; Tel. 265-7103. Famous business/translation school. 19 foreign teachers. (JIJ).

* IUE Eigo Gakuin, Kobayashi Bldg., 2-8-1 Minami Ikebukuro, Toshima-ku, Tokyo 171 Tel. 983-5466.

* Iwata Shokai; Tokyo, Nishi Shinjuku 3-5; (new); Tel. 343-0247.

* Japan Foreign Language Service, Ishikatsu Bldg., Minami Aoyama, Minato-ku, Tokyo; Tel. 479-2191.

* JEL Eigo Gakuin, 7-3 Todoroki, Setagaya-ku, Tokyo; Tel. 702-3828.

* Jido English School; Tokyo, Chuo-ku, Nihonbashi, Muro Ebiya Bldg.; (new); Tel. 243-1960.

* Jishu School; Tokyo, Toyoshima-ku, Higashi Ikebukuro 1-17; (new); Tel. 983-3483.

* Jiyu Foreign Language Center, Azusa Bldg., Todoroki, Setagaya-ku, Tokyo; Tel. 702-6771.

* Jiyu Language Center; Tokyo, Meguro-ku, Jiyugaoka 1-13; (new); Tel. 723-3130.

* JPS Academy, Jingumae 6-31, Shibuya-ku, Tokyo; Tel. 406-5555. Highly accelerated classes.

* JPS Academy; 150, Tokyo, Shibuya-ku, Shibuya Home 1308, Udagawa-cho 2-1; Tel. 464-5555. 20 foreign teachers. (JIJ).

* Jugaoka Language School; 152, Tokyo, Meguro-ku, Jugaoka Depato, Jugaoka 1-28-8, Tel. 718-3926. 10 foreign teachers. (JIJ).

* Jumi Eigo Kai, 4-41 Sakuradai, Nerima-ku, Tokyo; Tel. 991-4548.

* Kaigai Bunka Center, Koei Bldg., 1-7-4 Uchikanda, Chiyoda-ku, Tokyo 101 Tel. 295-4110.

* Kaminoge Road Gakuin, Tamaya Bldg., Kaminoge, 2-5-21 Setagaya-ku, Tokyo 165 Tel. 704-4367. .

* Kanda Gijitsu Academia, Morikyo Bldg. 1-2-9 Yoyogi, Shibuya-ku, Tokyo 151; Tel. 379-1795. Uses the direct method of instruction. (JIJ).

* Kanda Institute of Foreign Languages; 101, Tokyo, 2-13-13 Uchikanda; Tel. 254-2731. Largest school. 5,500 students, 94 foreign instructors. (JIJ).
* Kanrakuzaka Hearing Room; Tokyo, Shinjuku-ku, Kanrakuzaka 6-73; (new); Tel. 267-2246.
* Kanrisha Yosei Gakko; 150, Tokyo, Nishi-Shimbashi 3-19-13, Tokyo Kensho Bldg.; Tel. 433-8351. 5 foreign teachers. (JIJ).
* Keio Center; Tokyo, Meguro, Jiyugaoka, Kameda Bldg.; (new); Tel. 723-9475.
* Keishin Language School; 182, Tokyo, Chofu-shi, Senkawa-cho 1-2; Tel. 300-6885. Small classes. 9 foreign teachers. (JIJ).
* Kelly's English Lab; Tokyo, Shibuya-ku, Ebisu, Nishi Ogawa Bldg.; (new); Tel. 496-2353.
* Kent Academy, Tokyo, Shibuya-ku, Hiroo 5-4; Tel. 442-2938. Their motto: "Face to Face.".
* Kent English School; Tokyo, Shibuya-ku, Ebisu, Minami 1-6; (new); Tel. 711-3903.
* Kent House; Tokyo, Tamagawa Denenchofu 1-14; (new); Tel. 721-5311.
* Kent School; 150, Tokyo, Shibuya-ku, Ebisu Minami 1-6-3; Tel. 713-7046. 16 foreign teachers. (JIJ).
* Keto English School; Tokyo, Setagaya-ku, Sakuragaoka 2-10; (new); Tel. 426-2890.
* Kilby Gakuin; 160, Tokyo, Shinjuku-ku, Nishi-Shinjuku 1-21-1, Myoho Bldg. 5F; Tel. 342-6001. Features singing and dance classes. 8 foreign teachers. (JIJ).
* KLG; Tokyo, Meguro 1-12; (new); Tel. 493-8863.
* Kodo Language School; Tokyo, Chiyoda-ku, Rokubancho 13-2; (new); Tel. 261-1971.
* Koei Gakuin Kamedo Kyoshitsu, Tamagawaya Bldg., Kamedo, Koto-ku, Tokyo; Tel. 684-4371.
* Koike Trading Management; Tokyo, Shinjuku-ku, Minami Moto 4-40; (new); Tel. 355-1621.
* Kokusai Bunkya Center; Tokyo, Nerima-ku, Toyodamakita 5-16; (new); Tel. 993-4321.
* Kokusai Bunkya Kyokai; Tokyo, Chiyoda-ku, Kudankita 1-9; (new); Tel. 265-1407.
* Kokusai Business College; 150, Tokyo, 3-17-2 Shibuya-ku, Kaneda Bldg.; Tel. 409-1981. Secretarial school with 10 foreign teachers. (JIJ).

* Kokusai Eigo Gakkoo, 1-29-5 Yoyogi, Shibuya-ku, Tokyo 151 Tel. 370-0571.

* Kokusai Eiken Center; 158, Tokyo, Setagaya-ku, Seda 1-19-2, Akira Mansion; Tel. 709-7688. All foreign teachers (10). (JIJ).

* Kokusai English School; Tokyo, Edogawa-ku, Higashi Komatsugawa 1-12; (new); Tel. 655-6680.

* Kokusai Gakuin, Riyobi Bldg. 3F, 2-10-11 Kajimachi, Kanda, Chiyoda-ku, Tokyo; Tel. 252-0956.

* Kokusai Gogaku Center; Tokyo, Taito-ku, Ueno Kawamura Bldg.; (new); Tel. 842-5737.

* Kokusai Kenshukai; Tokyo, Chuo-ku, Ginza, Daini Namiya Bldg.; (new); Tel. 572-3166.

* Kokusai Kyoiku Kabu, Totoru Bldg., Higashi Azabu, Tokyo; Tel. 586-5331.

* Kokusai Renmei, Chisanamu Peidai, 24-8 Sakuragaoka-cho, Shibuya-ku, Tokyo 150 Tel. 496-2041. Primarily translation and inter-preting classes. .

* Kokusai Ryugaku Center; Tokyo, Shibuya, Oyama Bldg.; (new); Tel. 986-0221.

* Kokusai Seinen Inkai; Tokyo, Chiyoda-ku, Nagata-cho, Sanno Grand Bldg.; (new); Tel. 592-0940.

* Kokusai Shinzen; Tokyo, Shibuya-ku, Nishiwara 3-37; (new); Tel. 466-3028.

* Kokusai Shuriman; Tokyo, Shinjuku, Sanei, Bonaflower Bldg.; (new); Tel. 355-1168.

* Komagata English School; Tokyo, Taito-ku, Komagata 2-3; (new); Tel. 844-8310.

* Korakuen English Center, Koraku 1-3, Bunkyo-ku, Tokyo 112 Tel. 811-2111. Teaches only British.

* Kubo Takao; Tokyo, Toyoshima-ku, Kamiikebukuro 3-44; (new); Tel. 916-1403.

* Kyodo Weston School, Yuwa Bldg., 2-3-12 Kitazawa, Setagaya-ku, Tokyo 155 Tel. 412-3065.

* Language Training Service; Tokyo, Minato-ku, Shinbashi, Sogo Bldg.; (new); Tel. 574-7032.

* Lauren Language School; Tokyo, Setagaya-ku, Sangenjaya 1-19; (new); Tel. 421-1852.

* LC Language Club, 3-16-19 Roppongi, Minato-ku, Tokyo; Tel. 584-2813.

* LIC; Tokyo, Shibuya-ku, Dogenzaka 2-15; (new); Tel. 476-1051.

* Lingua Gakuin, Yuki Bldg. 3-303, 2-19-1 Koenji Minami, Suginami-ku, Tokyo 166; Tel. 312-2377. Small school with 2 foreign teachers. (JIJ).

* Linguarama; Akasaka Heights #401, 9-5-26 Akasaka, Minato-ku, Tokyo 107; Tel. 403-5724. All foreign teachers (9) offer assortment of classes. (JIJ).

* Lombard School, Yajima Bldg., Yotsuya, Shinjuku-ku, Tokyo; Tel. 358-6692.

* LS Language Study, 2-24 Kami Osaki, Shinagawa-ku, Tokyo; Tel. 493-0837.

* Lutheran School; 1-2-32 Fujimi, Chiyoda-ku, Tokyo 102; Tel. 263-9835. American Lutheran Church. 10 foreign teachers. (JIJ).

* Mary Pearl English School; Toyoshima-ku, Higashi Ikebukuro, Kaneko Bldg.; (new); Tel. 982-1938.

* Matsudo Eikaiwa, Kurokawa Bldg. 5F, 3-4 Sakuragaoka-cho, Shibuya-ku, Tokyo 150; Tel. 496-0555. Has own method, stressing "mental attitude." (JIJ).

* Matsumoto Eigo Semmon Gakkoo, Shibuya 1-4-8, Shibuya-ku, Tokyo 150; Tel. 400-8321. 5 foreign teachers use "spartan" approach to learning. (JIJ).

* Matsumoto English School; Tokyo, Shibuya 1-4; (new); Tel. 499-3381.

* Matsumoto English School; Tokyo, Suginami-ku, Onya 1-17; (new); Tel. 317-5316.

* McNall Foreign Language Gakuin, Shimada Bldg., Minami Koiwa, Edogawa-ku, Tokyo; Tel. 672-0201.

* Meguro Conversation Gakuin, 4-3 Kami Osaki, Shinagawa-ku, Tokyo; Tel. 493-7203.

* Meguro English Classroom, 5-22 Shirogane-dai, Minato-ku, Tokyo; Tel. 440-1921.

* Meguro School, Itaki Bldg. 3F, 2-15-15 Kamiosaki, Shinagawa-ku, Tokyo 141; Tel. 446-2181. Small classes for 5 foreign teachers. (JIJ).

* Meizen Gakuin, English School, 4-20 Kita Omori, Tokyo; Tel. 761-1124.

* Mesenkai Culture Center; Tokyo, Shinjuku-ku, Minami Moto 6-2; (new); Tel. 351-0297.

* Metro Gakuin, 1-18 Ichiyada, Tokyo; Tel. 260-6122.

* Mia American School; 162, Tokyo, Shinjuku-ku, Sumiyoshi-cho 108, OSK Bldg. 701; Tel. 358-1475. 10 foreign teachers. (JIJ).

* Mia Creative Academy, Edogawa-ku, Tokyo; Tel. 687-4896.

* Milestone Organization; Tokyo, Shibuya-ku, Jingumae 4-31; (new); Tel. 423-2551.

* Mimizuku English School; Tokyo, Shibuya-ku, Uehara 3-4; (new); Tel. 468-6818.

* Miniko; Nakao Bldg. 1-29-8 Komagome, Toshima-ku, Tokyo 170. Tel. 945-1691. (JIJ).

* Mita English Gakuin, 5-17 Komazawa, Setagaya-ku, Tokyo; Tel. 704-4947.

* Model Language Studio, Yasuto Bldg. 1-43-7 Yoyogi, Shibuya-ku, Tokyo 151; Tel. 370-7843. Stresses "live" English. 3 foreign teachers. (JIJ).

* Myosenkai Culture Center; 160, Tokyo, Shinjuku-ku, Minami Motomachi 6-2; Tel. 351-0297. All foreign teachers (15). (JIJ).

* Naganuma School, 16-26 Nanpeidai, Shibuya-ku, Tokyo 150 Tel. 463-7261.

* Nakajima Eigo Semmon Kyoshitsu, Nakaya Bldg., Shin Koiwa, Katsushikaku, Tokyo; Tel. 651-6791.

* NASA; 160, Tokyo, Shinjuku-ku, Takadano-baba 2-14-5; Tel. 200-9731. 5 foreign teachers. (JIJ).

* NCB, Shinjuku Center Bldg., 1-25-1 Nishi-Shinjuku, Shinjuku-ku, Tokyo 160 Tel. 342-5335.

* Nichibei Kaiwa Gakuin, Yotsuya 1-21, Shinjuku-ku, Tokyo 160; Tel. 359-9621. Prestigious school. 65 instructors, Ameri-can English. (JIJ).

* Nicholai Gakkuin, 4-1 Surugadai, Kanda, Chiyoda-ku, Tokyo 101; Tel. 291-9057. Founded in 1873. (JIJ).

* Nihon Business School, 6-7-13 Minami Aoyoma, Minato-ku, Tokyo 107; Tel. 400-2141. Teaches secretarial/trading skills, 110 foreign teachers. (JIJ).

* Nihon Gakuin Tsugakubu, Sohyo Kaikan 3F, 3-2-11 Surugadai, Kanda, Tokyo-to; Tel. 251-4735. Translation school with small foreign teaching staff (2). (JIJ).

* Nihon Gakuin; 162, Tokyo, Shinjuku-ku, Agebacho 20, Daini Tobundo Bldg.; Tel. 267-1331. 20 foreign teachers. (JIJ).

* Nihon Kagaku Honyaku Kyokai, Haruki Bldg., Kita Aoyama, Minato-ku, Tokyo; Tel. 403-8811.

* Nihon Kenkyujo; 160, Tokyo, Shibuya-ku, Yoyogi 2-23-1, New State Manor 1172; Tel. 370-3454. 18 foreign teachers. (JIJ).

* Nihon Kyoiku System; Tokyo, Shinjuku-ku, Nishi Shinjuku Toyo Bldg.; (new); Tel. 348-7951.

* Nihon Kyokai; Tokyo, Toyoshima-ku, Higashi Ikebukuro, Osumi Bldg.; (new); Tel. 986-3689.

* Nihon Resco; Tokyo, Shibuya-ku, Yoyogi 1-28; (new); Tel. 374-2721.

* Nihon Tsuyaku Yoseijo; 152, Tokyo, Shinagawa-ku, Kamiosaki 3-1-5, Eki Bldg. 8F; Tel. 440-4651. 8 foreign teachers for primarily translation students. (JIJ).

* Nino Carter Academy; Tokyo, Minato-ku, Akasaka 3-11; (new); Tel. 587-1941.

* Nippori Language Center; Tokyo, Arakawa-ku, Nishi Nippori 4-21-3; (new); Tel. 824-2401.

* Nishiyama Kikuko Eigo Kyoshitsu, 5-20 Higashi Koiwa, Edogawa-ku, Tokyo; Tel. 671-5282.

* Nisseito English Center; Tokyo, Adachi-ku, Aoi 4-1; (new); Tel. 848-3217.

* Nisseito; Tokyo, Toyoshima-ku, Mejiro 3-17; (new); Tel. 950-1111.

* Novice Foreign Language Gakuin, Sky Bldg., Kita Aoyama, Minato-ku, Tokyo; Tel. 404-8888.

* NSS Gaigo Gakuin, 6-13 Akasaka, Tokyo; Tel. 586-2997.

* Obunsha LL Kyoshitsu, 3-32 Narimasu, Itabashi-ku, Tokyo; Tel. 939-5703.

* Ogami English School; Tokyo; (new); Tel. 623-0863.

* Omura Gaigo Gakuin, Hongo Medical Bldg., Bunkyo-ku, Tokyo; Tel. 816-1761.

* Ono English School, 9-18 Kita Karasuyama, Setagaya-ku, Tokyo; Tel. 307-0509.

* Orikon English School; Tokyo, Chuo-ku, Ginza, Suyoroya Bldg.; (new); Tel. 571-6049.

* OSCC; 101, Tokyo, Chiyoda-ku, Kanda, 2-1 Surugadai; Tel. 291-1285. Emphasizes Bible teaching. All foreign teachers (10). (JIJ).

* Otani Chifumi; Tokyo, Shinagawa-ku, Osaki 4-1; (new); Tel. 492-4053.

* OTC; Tokyo, Chuo-ku, Yaesu Kotobuki Bldg.; (new); Tel. 275-0341.

* Oyama English School; Tokyo, Minato-ku, Moto Azabu 3-1; (new); Tel. 403-8950.
* PACC, Dai San Shikakura Bldg., 1-7 Yotsuya, Shinjuku-ku, Tokyo 160 Tel. 353-1771.
* Pacific English Club, 1-29 Hamadayama, Suginami-ku, Tokyo; Tel. 303-6764.
* Pacific Language School, 2-29 Higashi Takaido, Suginami-ku, Tokyo; Tel. 334-2849.
* Pacific Language School, Hikaru Bldg., Komaba, Meguro-ku, Tokyo; Tel. 465-9909.
* Pan Academic School; Tokyo, Shibuya-ku, Jingumae 1-17; (new); Tel. 478-5140.
* Pan World; Tokyo, Setagaya-ku, Seijo 2-40; (new); Tel. 416-2391.
* Panalingua, 1-43 Yoyogi, Tokyo; Tel. 370-7105.
* PE American Club, Ogikubo Bldg. 9F, 5-27-8 Ogikubo, Suginami-ku, Tokyo 167 Tel. 393-4391.
* Pearl English School; Tokyo; Nakano-ku, Matsugaoka 1-3; (new); Tel. 389-7347.
* Peck English Salon; Tokyo, Shinjuku, Shinjuku HK Bldg.; (new); Tel. 356-1312.
* Pegasus Language Service, Sankei Bldg. Shinkan, Ote, Tokyo; Tel. 244-4247.
* Pentagon English School; Tokyo, Shibuya, Miyano Bldg.; (new); Tel. 409-7200.
* PGK English Lounge; Tokyo, Nakano 5-52; (new); Tel. 385-7011.
* Pinocchio English Conversation Classroom, 6-8 Ikegami, Tokyo; Tel. 752-0361.
* Prade House; Tokyo, Minato-ku, Akasaka, New Akasaka Bldg.; (new); Tel. 584-2561.
* Prade House; Tokyo, Minato-ku, Akasaka 3-2; (new); Tel. 584-2569.
* Prade House; Tokyo, Toyoshima-ku, Higashi Ikebukuro 3-2; (new); Tel. 989-8135.
* Progre, Sanwa Bldg., Fujimi, Chiyoda-ku, Tokyo; Tel. 262-0087.
* Queen's English Conversation School, Okayama Bldg., 3-33-7 Kita Senaoku, Tokyo; Tel. 728-2351.
* Renaissance Eigo Gakuin; 150, Tokyo, Shibuya 1-24-7, Miyashita Park Bldg.; Tel. 407-8466. 5 foreign teachers. (JIJ).

* Richard Conversation Seminar, 2-48-12 Denen Chofu, Ota-ku, Tokyo; Tel. 721-3206.
* Ripitomeku School; 160, Tokyo, Shinjuku-ku, Shinano-cho 34, Toshin Bldg. 2F; 6 foreign instructors emphasize listening and speaking. (JIJ).
* Robert Gaigo Gakuin; 151, Tokyo, Shibuya-ku, Sendagaya 3-61-7; Tel. 401-0067. 25 foreign teachers. (JIJ).
* Robert's English Center; Tokyo, Setagaya-ku, Sangenjaya 1-39; (new); Tel. 424-9765.
* Royal English Seminar, 2-16 Todoroki, Setagaya-ku, Tokyo; Tel. 702-1824.
* Runashian Academy, 3-9 Umejima, Adachi-ku, Tokyo; Tel. 887-4510.
* Saimaru Academy; 106, Tokyo, Minato-ku, 1-5-17 Roppongi; Tel. 582-9841. 20 foreign teachers. Emphasizes simultaneous transla-tion. (JIJ).
* Salon Academy; 151, Tokyo, Shibuya-ku, Yoyogi 2-6-7, Seichi Bldg. 4F; Tel. 379-5661. All foreign teachers (15). (JIJ).
* San Luis Language Center, 2-15 Dogenzaka, Shibuya-ku, Tokyo; Tel. 464-9165.
* Sankei International College, 1-7-2 Shimbunsha Honkan, Otemachi, Tokyo 100 Tel. 246-0634. Classes are transferable to certain US universities.
* Sankei International College; 152, Tokyo, Meguro-ku, Hibumidani 5-9-8; Tel. 794-1761. 10 foreign teachers. (JIJ).
* SDA; 167, Tokyo, Suginami-ku, Tensho 3-17-3; Tel. 392-0419. All foreign teachers (11). (JIJ).
* Seijo School; Tokyo, Setagaya-ku, Seijo 2-8; (new); Tel. 416-4136.
* Shane English School; Tokyo, Edogawa-ku, Nishi Kuzunishi, Amafuji Bldg.; (new); Tel. 689-4143.
* Shane English School; Tokyo, Shibuya-ku, Ebisu Nishi 1-8; (new); Tel. 463-1064.
* Shenandoah Eigo Juku, 1-39 Minami Tokiwadai, Itabashi-ku, Tokyo; Tel. 956-4542.
* Shibuya Gaigo Gakuin; 150, Tokyo, Shibuya-ku, Sakuragaoka-cho 15-15; Tel. 461-8854. 8 foreign teachers. (JIJ).
* Shimada Eikaiwa Kenkyujo; 171, Tokyo, Toyoshima-ku, Minami-Nagasaki 1-14-8; Tel. 952-0061. Specializes in voice training. 1 foreign teacher. (JIJ).

* Shinagawa Foreign Language School, 3-25 Takanawa, Minato-ku, Tokyo; Tel. 447-7550.

* Shinjuku Kyoiku Kaikan, 7-22 Nishi Shinjuku, Tokyo; Tel. 363-1641.

* Shiragiku School; Tokyo, Itabashi-ku, Toshin 2-3; (new); Tel. 958-7171.

* Shuwa English School, 1-17 Sugamo, Toshima-ku, Tokyo; Tel. 947-9945.

* Simulax; Tokyo, Shibuya-ku, Sendagaya, Kagaku Kogyosha Bldg.; (new); Tel. 423-0281.

* SLS; Tokyo, Minato-ku, Roppongi, Maki Bldg.; (new); Tel. 582-9948.

* SMI; Tokyo, Shinjuku 1-9; (new); Tel. 356-1977.

* Smith-Okayama English Conversation School, 2-4 Okayama, Meguro-ku, Tokyo; Tel. 717-5907.

* Sokusei Iris Kyoshitsu, Residence Bldg., Kamiosaki Shuwa, Shinagawa-ku, Tokyo. Tel.445-1994. Many types of English classes taught.

* Sony Eigo Kyoshitsu; 160, Tokyo, Kurihara Bldg. 7F, 1-6-12 Nishi Shimbashi; Tel. 232-0290. Affiliated with Sony Corp. 40 unionized foreign teachers. (JIJ).

* Sony LL Shibuya, Kami Minami Bldg., 4-3 Udagawa-cho, Shibuya-ku, Tokyo; Tel. 461-9257.

* Sophia English Gakuin, 2-42 Minami Otsuka, Toshima-ku, Tokyo; Tel. 947-9317.

* SSS, 3-22 Aobadai, Meguro-ku, Tokyo; Tel. 793-5730.

* SSS, Hongo, Bunkyo-ku, Tokyo; Tel. 815-5844.

* SSS Institute, 10-9 Kami Izumi, Shibuya-ku, Tokyo; Tel. 496-5730.

* SSS, Soma Bldg., Kamiuma, Setagaya-ku, Tokyo; Tel. 424-6032.

* SSS, Toto Bldg., Higashi Ikebukuro, Tokyo; Tel. 988-6032.

* Stanton School of English; 102, Tokyo, Chiyoda-ku, Rokuban-cho 7; Tel. 262-3300. All British teachers (30) with TEFL license. (JIJ).

* Study Corner, Yutaka Bldg., Shimo Takaido, Suginami-ku, Tokyo; Tel. 322-1787.

* Successful English School, Towa Bldg., 515 Higashi Oizumi, Nerima-ku, Tokyo 188 Tel. 923-7249.

* Sun Academy, 1-4 Minami Akabane, Tokyo; Tel. 903-3764.

* Sun Language School; Tokyo, Shibuya 3-25; (new); Tel. 407-7423.

* Sun Life; 160, Tokyo, Shinjuku-ku, Takadanobaba 4-11-13, Art Daiichi Bldg. 2F; Tel. 367-4881. 20 foreign teachers. (JIJ).

* Sunbright Telephone Group; 105, Tokyo, Minato-ku, Shiba 3-22-7, CBC Bldg.; Tel. 451-1851. Lessons given by telephone, 34 teachers. (JIJ).

* Sundai ELS Eigo Gakuin; 101, Tokyo, Chiyoda-ku, Kanda, 1-5-8 Surugadai; Tel. 233-2311. Part of the world-wide ELS chain. 9 foreign teachers. (JIJ).

* Sunshine Business Gakko; 170, Tokyo, Toyoshima-ku, Higashi Ikebukuro 4-23-4; Tel. 987-5611. 14 foreign teachers. School emphasizes business courses. (JIJ).

* Sunshine Gaigo Gakko; 170, Tokyo, Higashi Ikebukuro 3-1-1, Sunshine Bldg. 9F; Tel. 987-1921. 5 foreign teachers. Relatively poor pay. (JIJ).

* Tatsunoko Culture Center, 3-16 Nishi Nippori, Tokyo; Tel. 824-4804.

* Terry's Children's Society, 3-30 Gohongi, Meguro-ku, Tokyo; Tel. 711-5004.

* TES; 103, Tokyo, Chuo-ku, Nihonbashi, Kodenba-cho 5-15; Tel. 663-8771. Business school with 12 foreign teachers. (JIJ).

* Tespa English Conversation School, 2-22 Kitazawa, Setagaya-ku, Tokyo; Tel. 414-4444.

* THE English School; Tokyo, Shibuya-ku, Jingumae 1-9; (new); Tel. 470-2457.

* Think Right English School; Tokyo, Shibuya-ku, Maruyama 15; (new); Tel. 461-4472.

* Thomas Gaigo Gakuin, 1-17 Jinbocho, Kanda, Chiyoda-ku, Tokyo; Tel. 291-9341.

* TIE English Conversation Club, 31 Sakuragaoka, Shibuya-ku, Tokyo; Tel. 496-6049.

* Time-Life Lang. Center, Time-Life Bldg. 1F, 2-3-6 Otemachi, Chiyoda-ku, Tokyo; Tel. 279-4370/270-6611.

* TIS, 1-3 Tsutsujigaoka, Chofu-shi, Tokyo; Tel. 307-4367.

* TOEFL Academy, New State Mena 2F, 2-23-1 Yoyogi, Shibuya-ku, Tokyo 151; Tel. 375-2307. 18 foreign teachers prepare students for the TOEFL exam. (JIJ).

* TOEFL Seminar; 160, Tokyo, Shinjuku-ku, Takadanobaba 4-13-10; Tel. 371-4391. 20 foreign teachers. (JIJ).

* Toho Gakuen Semmon Gakkoo, 2-4-1 Izumi, Suginami-ku, Tokyo 168; Tel. 323-8531. Affiliated with San Francisco Univ. 4 foreign teachers. (JIJ).

* Tokyo Academy; 141, Tokyo, Shinagawa-ku, Kamiosaki 2-15-14, Takagi Bldg. 5F; Tel. 440-7227. All foreign teachers (14). (JIJ).

* Tokyo Business College, Paris Saido Bldg. 1F, Hitotsubashi 1-1-1, Tokyo 100; Tel. 213-0962. Business school for import/-export. 8 foreign teachers. (JIJ).

* Tokyo English Conversation School, 3-20 Nishi Arai, Adachi-ku, Tokyo; Tel. 853-2501.

* Tokyo English Community Center; Tokyo, Shinjuku-ku, Takadanobaba 2-14-27; (new); Tel. 207-4421.

* Tokyo English House; Tokyo, Suginami-ku, Shoan 3-17; (new); Tel. 332-0940.

* Tokyo English House; Tokyo, Nakano-ku, Minamidai 3-46; (new); Tel. 384-0918.

* Tokyo Foreign Language Gakuin, Taguchi Bldg., Tomioka, Koto-ku, Tokyo; Tel. 641-5789.

* Tokyo Foreign Language College; 7-3-8 Nishi Shinjuku, Shinjuku-ku, Tokyo 160; Tel. 367-1101. Has a large foreign teaching staff (46). (JIJ).

* Tokyo Jido Gakuin; Tokyo, Chiyoda-ku, Kanda, Sakuma Sankyo Bldg.; (new); Tel. 866-8915.

* Tokyo Julius Gakuin, Kobayashi Dai Ni Bldg., Ningyo, Nihonbashi, Tokyo; Tel. 668-5636.

* Tokyo Kogakuin Gaigo Gakkoo; 161, Tokyo, Shinjuku-ku, Shimo-ochiai 1-1-8; Tel. 360-0341. 9 foreign teachers. Prefers British with experience. (JIJ).

* Tokyo Kokusai Gakuen Mejiro-ko, 3-20 Shimo Ochiai, Shinjuku-ku, Tokyo; Tel. 954-1797.

* Tokyo Language Center; Tokyo, Shibuya, Sanshin Bldg.; (new); Tel. 486-7661.

* Tokyo Language Center; Tokyo; Chuo-ku, Ginza, Dai Nichi Bldg.; (new); Tel. 543-6830.

* Tokyo School of Business; Yoyogi 1-56, Shibuya-ku, Tokyo 151; Tel. 370-2222. Emphasizes business ESL. 5 foreign teachers. (JIJ).

* Tokyo Suginami Eigo Gakko; 166, Tokyo, Suginami-ku, Koenji Minami 4-44-12; Tel. 314-2435. 4 foreign students. (JIJ).

* Tokyo Yamanote YMCA Eigo Gakoin, 2-18-12 Nishi Waseda, Shinjuku-ku, Tokyo 160. 9 foreign teachers use "living English" with role play and conversation. (JIJ).

* Tokyo YMCA Eigo Semmon Gakkoo, Mitoyo-cho 7, Kanda, Chiyoda-ku, Tokyo 101; Tel. 293-9471. Emphasizes culture and customs. 34 foreign teachers. (JIJ).

* Tokyo YWCA Semmon Gakkoo, 1-8 Surugadai, Kanda, Chiyoda-ku, Tokyo 101; Tel. 293-5421. 18 foreign teachers instruct mostly female students. (JIJ).

* Tommy Uematsu Language Center, 2-23 Yoyogi, Tokyo; Tel. 374-5055.

* Travel Journal Ryokoo Gakkoo, 4-6-6 Higashi Nakano, Nakano-ku, Tokyo 164; Tel. 367-8111. Travel school with 9 foreign teachers. (JIJ).

* Trendom, 2-5-4 Nishi Ebisu, Shibuya-ku, Tokyo; Tel. 464-0077.

* Trendom; Tokyo, Shibuya-ku, Ebisu, Minami Wakaba Bldg.; (new); Tel. 792-3321.

* Tsuda School of Business; 1-18-24 Sendagaya, Shibuya-ku, Tokyo 151; Tel. 402-7331. Business-oriented curriculum. 14 foreign teachers. (JIJ).

* Tsutsujigaoka Gaigo Gakuin, Sasaki Bldg., Tsutsujigaoka, Higashi Fuchu, Tokyo; Tel. 308-4302.

* Tsuyaku Gaido Yoseijo; 171, Tokyo, Toshima-ku, Takada 3-36-1; Tel. 988-6141. Emphasizes translation training. 30 foreign teachers. (JIJ).

* Tsuyaku Guide; Tokyo, Shinjuku-ku, Takadanobaba SKH Bldg.; (new); Tel. 200-4011.

* TT Conversation; Tokyo, Shinjuku-ku, Araki 11; (new); Tel. 351-5908.

* Turner English Conversation School, Mikado Bldg., Otsuka, Bunkyo-ku, Tokyo; Tel. 944-2951.

* Uni College; 101, Tokyo, Chiyoda-ku, Kanda, Jinbocho 1-19, Narita Bldg.; Tel. 291-7630. 3 foreign teachers. (JIJ).

* Universal Japan; Tokyo, Chuo-ku, Ginza, Mifuku Bldg.; (new); Tel. 561-6467.

* Universal Sangyo Gogaku Kenkyujo, Fujibo Kaikan, Fujimi, Chiyoda-ku, Tokyo; Tel. 234-5071.

* USA Information Center; Tokyo, Shibuya-ku, Jingumae 1-2; (new); Tel. 408-2901.
* Valentine Road English School, Ishizawa Bldg., Jiyugaoka, Meguro-ku, Tokyo; Tel. 724-6543.
* Warwick English Conversation School, 1-3 Nishi Azabu, Tokyo; Tel. 479-4545.
* Washington English Academy, Kugayama Bldg., Kugayama, Suginami-ku, Tokyo; Tel. 332-1258.
* Watson English Kenshujo, Matsuhide Bldg., Koishikawa, Bunkyo-ku, Tokyo; Tel. 947-0745.
* WCL Eifutsu Gogakuin, 3-7-4 Mejiro, Toshima-ku, Tokyo; Tel. 953-5930.
* West Eikaiwa Gakuin, 7-5 Akatsuka, Itabashi-ku, Tokyo; Tel. 938-2906.
* West Virginia University; 102, Tokyo, Chiyoda-ku, Gobancho 4-2, Topre Bldg.; Tel. 234-0357. All foreign teachers (10). (JIJ).
* Will English School; Tokyo, Minato-ku, Shiba 2-5; (new); Tel. 454-7737.
* Williams Academy; 150, Tokyo, Shibuya-ku, Jingumae 6-5-3, Ga-Z Bldg. 4F; Tel. 486-1248. 12 foreign teachers. (JIJ).
* WINS; 160, Tokyo, Shinjuku-ku, Nishi-Shinjuku 2-1-1, Mitsui Bldg. 49F; Tel. 344-4882. 14 foreign teachers. (JIJ).
* World English School; Tokyo, Adachi-ku, Nishi Arai, Hon 1-17; (new); Tel. 854-5475.
* World Languages Gakuin, Tokiwa Sogo Bldg., Kamiminami, Shibuya-ku, Tokyo; Tel. 464-1161.
* Yaesu School; Tokyo, Chuo-ku, Yaesu, Sumitomo Seimei Yaesu Bdlg.; (new); Tel. 274-3051.
* Yamaoka International, 5426 Oizumi Gakuen, Nerima-ku, Tokyo; Tel. 923-8888.
* Yamaoka International Academy, 3-12 Kita Aoyama, Minato-ku, Tokyo; Tel. 406-3144.
* Yamate American English Conversation Gakuin, 2-29 Ohara, Setagaya-ku, Tokyo; Tel. 328-3558.
* Yamate Eikaiwa School, 2-19-18 Shibuya, Shibuya-ku, Tokyo 150; Tel. 400-5025. Small classes. All foreign teachers (10). (JIJ).
* York English School; Tokyo, Toyoshima-ku, Higashi Ikebukuro 3-15; (new); Tel. 984-0360.

* York Kenkyujo; Tokyo, Meguro-ku, Kakinokizaka 2-15; (new); Tel. 718-6330.

* Yoshida English Classroom, 3-26 Nishi Ochiai, Shinjuku-ku, Tokyo; Tel. 951-0528.

* Yoshida English Center; Tokyo, Shinjuku-ku, Nishi Ochibori 2-15; (new); Tel. 951-0355.

* Yotsuya Gaigo Gakuin, PL Yotsuya Bldg., Motoshio-cho 9, Shinjuku-ku, Tokyo 160; Tel. 341-1434. Stresses "practical" Eng-lish. 20 foreign instructors. (JIJ).

* Yoyogi Mariko, 2-2 Asagaya Kita, Suginami-ku, Tokyo; Tel. 338-3044.

* Zora Language Center, 1-21 Jingumae, Shibuya-ku, Tokyo; Tel. 402-8649.

KANTO AREA

* AES; 243, Kanagawa-ken, Atsugi-shi, Nakamachi 3-18-14; Tel. 0462-24-3511. All foreign teachers (20). (JIJ).

* Asahi Culture Center; 220, Kanagawa-ken, Yokohama-shi, Nishi-ku, Takashima 2-16-1, Yokohama Lumine Bldg.; Tel. 045-453-1122. 40 foreign teachers. (JIJ).

* Berlitz School, Sky Bldg. 6F, 5-203 Motomachi, Naka-ku, Yokohama 231; Tel. 045-651-2891. See description of Berlitz above. (JIJ).

* Chiba YMCA Eigo Gakuin, Chiba, Masago 5-20-5; Tel. 0472-79-8411. 3 foreign teachers. (JIJ).

* Cosmos Gogaku Center; 221, Kanagawa-ken, Yokohama-shi, Kanagawa-ku, Nishi-Kanagawa 1-3-6, Coop Fuji 605; Tel. 045-321-2621. 2 foreign teachers. (JIJ).

* Cosmopolitan; 220, Yokohama, Nishi-ku 2-11-2, Sky Manor 405; Tel. 045-453-2620. Small school with one foreign teacher. (JIJ).

* Designer Gakuin; 220, Yokohama, Kanagawa-ku, Daimachi 22-14; 3 foreign teachers. Emphasizes hotel and travel English. (JIJ).

* East-West Gaikokugo Semmon Gakko; 281, Chiba, Inagedai-cho 18-10; Tel. 0472-43-7611. 4 foreign teachers. (JIJ).

* English House Gakuin, 4-22-1 Chiyogaoka, Kawasaki-shi 215; Tel. 044-955-0809. 5 foreign teachers. (JIJ).

* Fujisawa Gaigo Center, Hirota Bldg. 2F & 3F, Fujisawa 976, Fujisawa-shi, Kanagawa-ken; Tel. 0466-26-0203. 19 foreign teachers emphasize speaking. (JIJ).

* Gaigo Business Semmon Gakko; 210, Kanagawa-ken, Kawasaki-shi, Eki Mae Honcho 22-9; Tel. 044-244-1959. 47 foreign teachers and broad curriculum. (JIJ).

* Gogaku Kenshu Center; 221, Kanagawa-ken, Yokohama-shi, Kanagawa-ku, Tsuruya-cho 3-32, Academia Bldg.; Tel. 045-311-5361. 35 foreign teachers. (JIJ).

* Hioshi Eigo Gakuin, 1778 Hiyoshi Hommachi, Kohoku-ku, Yokohama 220; Tel. 044-61-7040. 4 foreign students. (JIJ).

* JCC Academy; 223, Yokohama, Minato Kita-ku, Hiyoshi Motomachi 1867-1, Hiyoshi Center Bldg. 3F; Tel. 044-63-6469. 2 foreign teachers. (JIJ).

* Kansai Gaigo Gakuin; 640, Wakayama, Nishi Takamatsu 1-5-1; Tel. 0734-36-5694. 2 foreign teachers. (JIJ).

* LIOJ; 250, Kanagawa-ken, Odawara-shi, Shiroyama 4-14-1, Asia Center Nai; Tel. 0465-23-1667. All foreign teachers (20). Training/experience required. (JIJ).

* Mobara Eigo Gakuin; 297; Chiba-ken, Mobara-shi, Takashi 619-11; Tel. 0475-22- 4785. Very small school with 1 foreign teacher. (JIJ).

* QE Eikaiwa Gakuin; 272, Chiba-ken, Ichikawa-shi, Minami Yawata 4-7-14, Yugetsu Bldg. 3F; Tel. 0473-77-1143. 6 foreign teachers. (JIJ).

* Seimei Bldg. 4F; Tel. 045-311-5803. 9 foreign teachers. (JIJ).

* Shonan English College, 1-2-2 Kobukuro-dai, Kamakura-shi, Kanagawa-ken 247; Tel. 0467-46-7370. 6 foreign teachers. (JIJ).

* Sony Eigo Kyoshitsu; 220, Yokohama, Kanagawa-ku, Tsuruya-cho 2-25-2, Mitsui Seimei Bldg. 4F; Tel. 045-311-5803. 9 foreign teachers. (JIJ).

* Yamate Eigakuin, 1-36 Hinode-cho, Naka-ku, Yokohama-shi, Kanagawa-ken; Tel. 045-231-1841. 3 foreign teachers. (JIJ).

* Yokohama Academy, Academy Bldg., Tsuruyakucho 3-32, Kanagawa-ku, Yokohama 221; Tel. 045-311-5361. Oldest secretarial school in Japan. 35 foreign teachers. (JIJ).

* Yokohama Gaigo Business College, Yamanote-cho 45, Naka-ku, Yokohama 231; Tel. 045-641-3919. Large business school. 11 foreign teachers. (JIJ).

* Yokohama YMCA Gakuin, 1-7 Joban-cho, Naka-ku, Yokohama 231; Tel. 045-662-3721. 24 foreign teachers. See YMCA description above. (JIJ).

CENTRAL HONSHU

* Colorado Eigo Gakuin; 676, Hyogo-ken, Takasago-shi, Yoneda-cho, Yonedashin 20-3; Tel. 0794-31-6507. 2 foreign teachers. (JIJ).

* English Center; 430, Shizuoka-ken, Hamamatsu-shi, Toshimachi 11, Kawai Bldg.; Tel. 0534-56-0109. 8 foreign teachers teach full range of courses. Negative report received from former teacher. Approach with caution. (JIJ).

* Hokoku Bunka Center; 920, Ishikawa-ken, Kanazawa-shi, Hondo-cho 3-2-1, MRO Bldg.; Tel. 0762-22-0101. 5 foreign teachers. (JIJ).

* ILC; 500, Gifu, Nagasumi-cho 1-14; Tel. 0582-63-3936. 2 foreign teachers. (JIJ).

* Ise Eigo Center; 516, Miye-ken, Iseshi, Kamihisa 1-4-11; Tel. 0596-28-7629. Old but small school with only one foreign teacher on a staff of 3. (JIJ).

* Life Academy; 518-04, Miye-ken, Nabari-shi, Kikyogaoka 4-5-69; Tel. 0595-65-0968. Features word processing training. 3 foreign teachers. (JIJ).

* Nagaoka Business Semmon Gakko; 940, Niigata-ken, Nagaoka-shi, Otedori 2-4-9; Tel. 0258-35-1055. 2 foreign teachers. (JIJ).

* Yamanashi YMCA; 400, Kofu, Chuo 5-4-11; Tel. 0552-35-8543. 7 foreign teachers. (JIJ).

* Nakamura Eigo School; 389-22, Nagano-ken; Iyama-shi, Fukuju-cho 1138; Tel. 0269-62-2835. 1 foreign teacher. (JIJ).

* Niigata Business Semmon Gakko; 950, Niigata, Bandai 1-1-22; Tel. 0252-41-2131. 6 foreign teachers. (JIJ).

* Nomado Gaigo Gakuin, Hattori Bldg. 3F, 3-2 Koyamachi, Shizuoka 420; Tel. 0542-55-8858. All foreign teachers (5). (JIJ).

* YMCA Gakuin; 670, Hyogo-ken, Himeji-shi, Tsuchiyama, Higashi No-cho 9-15; Tel. 0792-98-5566. 2 foreign teachers. (JIJ).

OSAKA AREA ("06" telephone prefix)

* Abeno English/Math School; Hariake 11-59, Abeno-ku, Osaka, (new); Tel. 653-5753.
* Abeno YMCA, Minami Kawabori 9, Tennoji-ku, Osaka 543; Tel. 779-8361.
* Access Systems; Umeda 1-1, Kita-ku, Osaka, (new); Tel. 343-2921.
* Ace English School; Urabae 4-21, Joto-ku, Osaka, (new); Tel. 939-2371.
* ACLA; Nakazaki Nishi 2-2, Kita-ku, Osaka, (new); Tel. 314-2267.
* Akashiya English Center; Nishi Tenman 3-5, Kita-ku, Osaka, (new); Tel. 365-8468.
* Akatsuka English School; Maruyama 1-1, Abeno-ku, Osaka, (new); Tel. 652-3399.
* ALI Iwai Beigo Gakkan, Kanaoka 3-20, Higashi Osaka 577; Tel. 720-3468.
* Ambic Eikaiwa School, Dai Yuji 8, Kita-ku, Osaka 530; Tel. 315-1601.
* Ambic; Nanba Sennichimae 15, Minami-ku, Osaka, (new); Tel. 644-6734.
* American English School, Higashi Sangoku 1-32, Yodogawa-ku, Osaka 532; Tel. 395-3009.
* Asahi Cultural Center; Nakanoshima 3-2, Kita-ku, Osaka, (new); Tel. 222-5222.
* AZ English School; Dairyo 4-4, Sumiyoshi-ku, Osaka, (new); Tel. 692-0034.
* Babel Gakuin; 530, Osaka, Kita-ku, Umeda 1-11-4, Osaka Ekimae Bldg.; Tel. 344-5111. 3 foreign teachers. (JIJ).
* Babel; Higashi Tenman 1-9, Kita-ku, Osaka, (new); Tel. 354-2079.
* Beacon Language Center; Hon 3-12, Higashi-ku, Osaka, (new); Tel. 943-8991.
* Berlitz School, Hotel Hanshin Bldg. 2F, 2-3-24 Umeda, Kita-ku, Osaka 530; Tel. 341-2531. (JIJ).
* Berlitz; Hon 2-5, Higashi-ku, Osaka, (new); Tel. 271-4662.

* Berlitz; Kita-ku, Osaka (new); Tel. 311-5631.
* Bilingual Osaka; 520, Osaka, Kita-ku, Sonezaki Shinji 2-3-4, Ekimae Bldg.; Tel. 344-1720. 170 foreign instructors in Bilingual chain. (JIJ).
* Bishop English School, 1-19 Higashi Noda, Toshima-ku, Osaka; Tel. 353-6798.
* Chiari English Kenkyukai; Nishi Tenman 4-11, Kita-ku, Osaka, (new); Tel. 363-0361.
* Chiari; Denpo 2-13, Konohana-ku, Osaka, (new); Tel. 463-3737.
* Cultural Communication Int'l; Nishi Nakajima 7, Yodogawa-ku, Osaka, (new); Tel. 305-4633.
* EBJ; Denpo 1-1, Konohana-ku, Osaka, (new); Tel. 468-8638.
* ECC Gaigo Gakkoo, 2-9 Higashi Noda, Toshima-ku, Osaka 530-91; Tel. 358-5904.
* ECC Osaka Gaigo Gakuin, 3-4 Shinchi, Sonezaki, Kita-ku, Osaka 530; Tel. 341-6759.
* ECC; 530, Osaka, Nakazaki Nishi 2-3-35; Tel. 373-0144. (JIJ).
* ECC; Abeno 1-6, Abeno-ku, Osaka, (new); Tel. 649-0731.
* ECC; Higashi Saka, Ashikaga 2-22, Higashi Osaka-shi, Osaka, (new); Tel. 729-5518.
* ECC; Jusanbon 1-5, Yodogawa-ku, Osaka, (new); Tel. 309-5235.
* ECC; Nanba 4-5, Minami-ku, (new); Tel. 633-7197.
* ECC; Umeda 2-2, Kita-ku, Osaka, (new); Tel. 341-3287.
* Echo Gaigo Gakuin, 2-1 Niimori, Asahi-ku, Osaka 535; Tel. 955-1109.
* ECP Eigo Kyoiku Center, 1-17 Minami Kishibe, Suita-shi, Osaka 564; Tel. 383-8691.
* Ekumi Eikaiwa School, 1-71 Naka Sonezaki, Kita-ku, Osaka 530; Tel. 312-7545.
* El Business Gakko; 556, Osaka, Naniwa-ku, Nanba-naka 3-13-1; Tel. 647-0011. 10 foreign teachers with hotel and tour guide classes. (JIJ).
* EM Gaigo Kenkyujo, 12-1 Hashizume, Uchihoncho, Higashi-ku, Osaka 594; Tel. 941-0134.
* English Academy; Shimanouchi 1-18, Minami-ku, Osaka, (new); Tel. 252-7316.

* English Academy, 1-40 Nishi Senriyama, Suita-shi, Osaka 565; Tel. 385-6555.
* English Academy, 2-8 Higashi Noda, Toshima-ku, Osaka 530-91; Tel. 351-6833.
* English Baret School; Imabuku Minami 2-12, Joto-ku, Osaka, (new); Tel. 393-5458.
* English Group, 2-12 Nakahama, Joto-ku, Osaka 530; Tel. 962-4812.
* English Space Academy; Sonezaki Shinchi 2-3, Kita-ku, Osaka, (new); Tel. 341-6460.
* English World, 1-5 Higashi Awashi, Higashi Yodogawa-ku, Osaka 533; Tel. 325-3431.
* ESO; Asahi 1-1, Abeno-ku, Osaka, (new); Tel. 649-2209.
* Esu English/Math School; Tezukayama 1-8, Abeno-ku, Osaka, (new); Tel. 653-0818.
* Esu Gakuin; Fukada 1-2, Kita-ku, Osaka, (new); Tel. 371-3069.
* Executive Gogaku Center; Nomura Bldg., 4-4-1 Hommachi, Higashi-ku, Osaka 541;
   Tel. 271-8978. 109 foreign teachers in Executive chain. (JIJ).
* Foreign Language Center; Nishikiyosui 8, Minami-ku, Osaka, (new); Tel. 242-1741.
* Gloria American Center; Shincho 1-3, Nishi-ku, Osaka, (new); Tel. 538-3091.
* Gogaku Foreign Language Center; Shibada 1-4, Kita-ku, Osaka, (new); Tel. 374-0615.
* Harrow Center; 532, Osaka, Yodogawa-ku, Nishi Nakajima 3-20-8, Shinwa Bldg.
   5F; Tel. 428-6241. All foreign teachers (10). (JIJ).
* Honmachi Academy; Hon 2-5, Higashi-ku, Osaka, (new); Tel. 262-3957.
* IEC Eigo Gakuin, 4-6 Higashi Nagai, Sumiyoshi-ku, Osaka 558; Tel. 696-3656.
* IF; 532, Osaka, Yodogawa-ku, Nishi Nakajima 1-9-20, Shin Nakashima Bldg. 7F; Tel. 305-0721. 7 foreign teachers special-ize in TOEFL/GMAT preparation. (JIJ).
* Ikuji Sunroom; Kamimasa Kakuji 4-5, Hirano-ku, Osaka, (new); Tel. 793-8124.
* Ikuno Foreign Language School; Shariji 3-15, Ikuno-ku, Osaka, (new); Tel. 741-8641.

* ILC; 530, Osaka, Kita-ku, Sumida-cho 8-47, Hankyu Grand Bldg. 24F; Tel. 315- 8003. All foreign teachers (15) British. Main office in London. (JIJ).

* Institue of Foreign Study, 1-9 Nishi Nakajima, Yodogawa-ku, Osaka 532; Tel. 305-3022.

* International Academy; Nanba 1-18, Naniwa-ku, Osaka, (new); Tel. 647-2331.

* Interworld Center; Naka Hon 2-7, Higashi-ku, Osaka, (new); Tel. 943-8991.

* James Language School; Tezukayama 1-23, Abeno-ku, Osaka, (new); Tel. 654-1600.

* James Language Service Eikaiwa, Togano 15, Kita-ku, Osaka 530; Tel. 315-8200.

* Junior English Center; Sogashi Higashi 3-1, Sumiyoshi-ku, Osaka, (new); Tel. 692-3847.

* Jusan Academy; Juso Higashi 2-2, Yodogawa-ku, Osaka, (new); Tel. 303-3538.

* Kansai English School, 1-27 Seigakuhon, Settsu-shi, Osaka 564; Tel. 382-6276.

* KEC; 573, Osaka-fu, Hirakata-shi, Nishi Kiino 2-4-17, Daigo Matsuba Bldg.; Tel. 0720-31-0616. 2 foreign teachers. (JIJ).

* Ken's Way; Tsukaguchi 1-21, Amagasaki-shi, Osaka, (new); Tel. 421-3513.

* Ken's Way; Tsuneyoshi Akada 1, Amagasaki-shi, Osaka, (new); Tel. 432-4474.

* Kinazu Eikaiwa, Shinko 3-9, Yodogawa-ku, Osaka 532; Tel. 393-4461.

* Kingston Eikaiwa Gakuin, Nishi Nakajima 1-12, Yodogawa-ku, Osaka 532; Tel. 304-0030.

* Kori Gaikokugo Center; 572, Osaka-fu, Neagawa-shi, Kori Nishino-cho 12-1; Tel. 0720-31-0616. 3 foreign teachers. (JIJ).

* Kuji Stewardess School; Nakazaki Nishi 2-2, Kita-ku, Osaka, (new); Tel. 361-3341.

* Maria Foreign Language Gakuin; Takakonoso 4-30, Amagasaki-shi, Osaka, (new); Tel. 433-2829.

* MEC; Nakano 4-12, Higashi Sumiyoshi-ku, Osaka, (new); Tel. 797-5757.

* Minami Moricho English School; Minami Mori 2-1, Kita-ku, Osaka, (new); Tel. 364-7307.

* Momoyama English Seminar; Showa 3-1, Abeno-ku, Osaka, (new); Tel. 621-0801.

* Nakamura Kyoshitsu; Minami Sumiyoshi 3-1, Sumiyoshi-ku, Osaka, (new); Tel. 695-5133.
* Nakayama English School; Sotojima 2-9, Moriguchi-shi, Osaka, (new); Tel. 991-4077.
* Nanba Foreign Language Center; Nanba Naka 2-8, Naniwa-ku, Osaka, (new); Tel. 633-1620.
* Naniwa Foreign Language Gakuin; Nagai Higashi 4-13, Sumiyoshi-ku, Osaka, (new); Tel. 697-1958.
* Naniwa Foreign Language School; Oimasato 3-16, Higashi Nari-ku, Osaka, (new); Tel. 975-1948.
* Naniwa Foreign Lang. School; Toyosato 5-11, Higashi Yodogawa-ku, Osaka, (new); Tel. 326-5758.
* Naniwa Foreign Language School; Kiren 2-7, Hirano-ku, Osaka, (new); Tel. 708-7288.
* Naniwa Gaigo Gakuin, 7-9 Takatsu-cho, Minamai-ku, Osaka 542; Tel. 641-5678.
* Naniwa School; Higashi Saka, Tsurike Moto 1-15, Higashi Osaka-shi, Osaka, (new); Tel. 745-6128.
* National LL School; Umeda 1-3, Kita-ku, Osaka, (new); Tel. 345-1272.
* NCB Eikaiwa Kyoshujo, Umeda 1-2, Kita-ku, Osaka 530; Tel. 345-5111/7111.
* Nichibei English School; Umeda 1-11, Kita-ku, Osaka, (new); Tel. 344-7702.
* Nichibei English School; Nanba 1-4, Minami-ku, Osaka, (new); Tel. 211-2032.
* Nichibei Enlish School; Asahi 1-1, Abeno-ku, Osaka, (new); Tel. 649-5039.
* Nichibei Tennojiko; Abenosuji 1-5, Abeno-ku, Osaka, (new); Tel. 631-7023.
* Nihon Business School, Miahara 4-4-65, Yodogawa-ku, Osaka 532; Tel. 391-0061. 4 foreign teachers. (JIJ).
* Nippon Eikaiwa Gakuin, Sumida 1, Kita-ku, Osaka 530; Tel. 312-3730/3667/3739.
* Osaka Eigo Academy, 3-7 Tenjinbashi, Kita-ku, Osaka 530; Tel. 354-1735.
* Osaka Eigo Gakkoo, 3-3 Kita-Horimachi, Tennojiku, Osaka 543; Tel. 771-7659. Stresses "free conversation practice.".
* Osaka Eikaiwa Gakkoo; 530, Osaka, Kita-ku, Nakanoshima 3-6, Osaka Bldg.; Tel. 441-9035. 4 foreign teachers. (JIJ).

* Osaka English Gakuin; Shigeta Omiya 4-2, Tsurumi-ku, Osaka, (new); Tel. 911-5680.

* Osaka Furitsu Boeki Semmon Gakko; 543, Osaka, Tennojiku, Yuhigaoka-cho 5; Tel. 942-2717. 2 foreign teachers. (JIJ).

* Osaka Gaigo Semmon Gakko; 540, Osaka, Higashi-ku, Shimamachi 2-5; Tel. 944-1061. 17 foreign teachers. (JIJ).

* Osaka YMCA College; 550, Osaka, Nishi-ku, Tosabori 1-5-6; Tel. 441-0892. 13 foreign teachers. Mostly tour guide and hotel classes. (JIJ).

* Osaka YMCA Gogaku Semmon Gakkoo, 1-4-13 Sonezaki Shinchi, Kita-ku, Osaka 550; Tel. 341-1701. Stresses public speaking and discussion.

* PL Foreign Language Gakuin; Shinsaibashi 1-48, Minami-ku, Osaka, (new); Tel. 241-9325.

* Rawhide English School; Minami Horie 1-11, Nishi-ku, Osaka, (new); Tel. 531-6340.

* Resta Language School, 2-1 Dojima, Kita-ku, Osaka 530; Tel. 344-2062/5131.

* Sankei International College, Sankei Bldg. 8F, Umeda 2-4-9, Kita-ku, Osaka 530; Tel. 347-0751. 8 foreign teachers. (JIJ).

* SDA, 1-40 Tani, Higashi-ku, Osaka 540; Tel. 941-1107.

* Semmon Gakko Tennoji Eigo Gakuin; 545; Osaka, Abeno-ku, Matsuzaki-cho 2-9-36; Tel. 623-1851. 11 foreign teachers. Recommended. (JIJ).

* Shibata Gakuin; Hama 1-1, Tsurumi-ku, Osaka, (new); Tel. 912-1838.

* Shin Nippon English School; Kita Sumiya 15, Minami-ku, Osaka, (new); Tel. 245-8090.

* Shogakkan Home English Center; Shibata 1-4, Kita-ku, Osaka, (new); Tel. 374-2371.

* Showa Esu Gakuin; Hanan 3-10, Abeno-ku, Osaka, (new); Tel. 623-4398.

* So English Kyoshitsu; Fuminosato 4-1, Abeno-ku, Osaka, (new); Tel. 628-2348.

* Sone English Club; Toyonaka Hama 1-4, Settsu-shi, Osaka, (new); Tel. 334-5960.

* Sony LL, Nishi Hankyu Bldg. 4F, Shibata 2-1-18, Kita-ku, Osaka 530; Tel. 372-6777.

* Takakonoso English Gakuin; Takeko 1-28, Amagasaki-shi, Osaka, (new); Tel. 437-1548.

* Tennoji English Gakuin; Daido 3-1, Tennoji-ku, Osaka, (new); Tel. 771-1882.

* Tennoji English/Math Gakuin; Horikoshi 10, Tennoji-ku, Osaka, (new); Tel. 771-4609.

* Tezukayama English Center, 3-8 Tezukayamanaka, Sumiyoshi-ku, Osaka 558; Tel. 678-2548/672-5720.

* Tokyo Foreign Language Center; Chaya 18, Kita-ku, Osaka, (new); Tel. 375-0361.

* Tomo English School; 530, Osaka, Kita-ku, Doshin 2-2-15, Sun Laurel 301; Tel. 352-0687. 3 foreign teachers. (JIJ).

* Tsurugaoka Eigo Club, 5-2 Yamazaka, Higashi Sumiyoshi-ku, Osaka 546; Tel. 696-3934.

* Uehara English Juku; Hanan 5-18, Abeno-ku, Osaka, (new); Tel. 623-7584.

* ULS English Kyoshitsu; Hanan 3-14, Abeno-ku, Osaka, (new); Tel. 623-2190.

* Umeda Gakuin Eigo Semmon Gakkoo, 2-30 Chayayamachi, Kita-ku, Osaka 530; Tel. 376-0661. Mostly adult students for 11 foreign teachers. (JIJ).

* Universal Gaigo Gakuin, 2-39 Azuchi, Higashi-ku, Osaka 541; Tel. 266-0395.

* World English Juku; Nishi Kawanomoto 1-61, Amagasaki-shi, Osaka, (new); Tel. 499-7119.

* World Language School; Umeda 1-3, Kita-ku, Osaka, (new); Tel. 341-6636.

* Yamatani English Gakuin; Takekonoso 1-3, Amagasaki-shi, Osaka, (new); Tel. 436-0685.

* YMCA Telephone Service; Takashima 1-5, Kita-ku, Osaka, (new); Tel. 341-2315.

* YMCA; Higashi Saka, Mishiku Minami 3-1, Higashi Osaka-shi, Osaka, (new); Tel. 787-3232.

* Yomiuri Gaigo Business Semmon, 2-5 Shima, Higashi-ku, Osaka 540; Tel. 944-1091.

* Yotsubashi English School; Kita Horie 1-10, Nishi-ku, Osaka, (new); Tel. 538-3096.

* YSF Eigo Kyoshitsu, Omiya 5-2, Asahi-ku, Osaka 535; Tel. 953-8665.

* YWCA Secretarial Arts School; 550, Osaka, Kita-ku, Kamiyama-cho 11-12; Tel. 361-0838. 8 foreign teachers. (JIJ).

KYOTO AREA

* Bi-Lingual English Conversation School; 605 Kyoto, Higashiyama-ku, Shijodori, Yamato-oji Nishi Iru, Nakanomachi 200, Kamogawa Bldg. 9F. "An expanding company" which has found JOBS IN JAPAN "valuable in that it has led many prospective teachers to our doorstep for interviews." (JIJ).

* ECC; 604, Kyoto, Nakagyo-ku, Karawamachi-dori, Shijo Agaru; Tel. 075-223-0196. (JIJ).

* Kyoto English Center, Sumitomo Seimei Bldg. 8F, Nishi Shijo Karasuma, Shimo Nyooku, Kyoto 600; Tel. 075-221-2251. Emphasizes extra-curricular activities with students and foreign teachers (45). (JIJ).

* Kyoto YMCA, Kado, Sanjo Yanagibajo, Nakagyo-ku, Kyoto 604; Tel. 075-231-4388. Together with next listing, 50 foreign teachers. (JIJ).

* Kyoto YMCA Semmon Gakkoo, Sagaru, Imadegawa Karasuma, Kamigyoku, Kyoto 602; Tel. 075-432-3191. Emphasizes practical business skills. (JIJ).

* Lake Gaigo Gakuin, Ikawa Hairu, Higashi Horikawa, Nakagyoku, Kyoto 604; Tel. 075-221-7686. Conversation stressed for 10 foreign teachers. (JIJ).

* Nara Gaigo Business Typist Gakuin; 634, Nara-ken, Kashihara-shi, Uchizen-cho 5-3-31, Fuji Bldg. 7F; Tel. 0744-22-7688. 3 foreign teachers. (JIJ).

* Riseikan Gaikuin; 663, Hyogo-ken, Nishinomiya-shi, Kitaguchi-cho 4-25; Tel. 0798-65-2011. 8 foreign teachers. (JIJ).

* SEI; 520, Shiga-ken, Otsu-shi, Kyomachi 3-2-6, Eiki Bldg. 3F; Tel. 0775-24-8879. 2 foreign teachers. (JIJ).

KOBE AREA ("078" telephone prefix)

* Anbik Gaigo Gakuin, Ikuta-ku, Kobe 650; Tel. 331-1561.

* Berlitz, Kyowa Bldg. 4F, 5-12-7 Shimoyamate-dori,, Chuo-ku, Kobe 650; Tel. 351-1583. (JIJ).

* Clara Gaigo School, 1-39 Nakayamate, Ikuta-ku, Kyoto 650; Tel. 241-3288.

* ECC, 1-1-1 Nishi Tachibanadori, Hyogo-ku, Kobe 652; Tel. 576-7758. 4 foreign teachers. See description of ECC earlier. (JIJ).

* ECC, Sannomiya 1-17, Ikuta-ku, Kobe 650; Tel. 321-2419.
* Executive School, Shokoboeki Center Bldg., 5-1-14, Hamabedori, Chuo, Kobe 651; Tel. 251-2412. See description of Executive earlier. (JIJ).
* Kobe YMCA, 2-7-15 Kanocho, Chuo-ku, Kobe 650; Tel. 241-7201. 5 foreign teachers. See description of YMCA earlier. (JIJ).
* Kokusai Business Gakuin, 5-3-5 Kotono Ocho, Chuo-ku, Kobe 651; Tel. 242-5178. Training for business/industry. 2 foreign teachers. (JIJ).
* KS Eikaiwa, 3-9-7 Sannomiya-cho, Chuo-ku, Kobe 650; tel. 391-8711; Tel. 391-8711. "KS" stands for "kindness and sincerity."
* Seinikaeru Kokusai Gakkoo, 3-17-2 Nakayamate-dori, Chuo-ku, Kobe 650; Tel. 221-8028. Trains students for Cambridge. 5 British instructors. (JIJ).
* Toa Gaigo Gakuin, Ikuta-ku, Kobe 650; Tel. 321-2339.

NAGOYA AREA

* Asahi Culture Center; 460, Aichi-ken, Nagoya, Naka-ku, Sakae 3-4-5, Marue Sky 10F; Tel. 052-261-3866. 2 foreign teachers. (JIJ).
* Nagoya Business Semmon Gakko, Denba 3-2-3, Atsuta-ku, Nagoya 456; Tel. 052-682-7879. 3 foreign students. (JIJ).
* Nagoya Gaikokugo Semmon Gakkoo; Imaike 1-5-31, Chikusaku, Nagoya 464; Tel. 741-2304. 20 foreign teachers teach mostly business classes. (JIJ).
* Nagoya International School, 2686 Minamihara, Nakashidami, Moriyama-ku, Nago-ya 463. Not an ESL school. Generally hires only experienced instructors with teaching credentials to teach general junior and high school curriculum. (JIJ).
* Nihon Business School, Mei Eki Minami 1-23-17, Nakamura-ku, Nagoya 450; Tel. 582-3026. 5 foreign teachers. (JIJ).
* Professional English Course; 461, Aichi-ken, Nagoya, Higashi-ku, Aori 1-25-1, Nishin Bldg. 508; Tel. 052-937-7339. 10 foreign teachers. (JIJ).

SHIKOKU ISLAND AREA

* Anbik School; 770, Tokushima, Terashima Honcho, Nishi Ichome, Awa Kendo Bldg. 5F; Tel. 0886-25-4291. 5 foreign teachers. (JIJ).
* Ehime Eigo Academy, 2-9-6 Ichiban-cho, Matsuyama-shi, Ehime-ken 790; Tel. 0899-31-8686. 7 foreign teachers. (JIJ).
* Takamatsu Nichibei Gakuin, 10-20 Marunouchi, Takamatsu-shi, Kagawa-ken 760; Tel. 0878-21-3382. 5 foreign teachers. (JIJ).

FUKUOKA AREA AND SOUTHERN JAPAN

* American Center; 880, Miyazaki, Hachiba-na-dori Higashi 5-3, Ono Bldg. 3F; Tel. 0985-53-4521. 2 foreign teachers feature role play and public speaking. (JIJ).
* Berlitz, Futaba Bldg. 7F, Tenjin 3-1, Chuo-ku, Fukuoka, 810; Tel. 751-9888. See Berlitz description earlier. (JIJ).
* Caine's Eikaiwa Typing School, 1-1 Maizuru, Chuo-ku, Fukuoka 810; Tel. 721-5020. 14 foreign teachers for business, vocational and general classes. (JIJ).
* ECC Gaigo Gakuin; 810, Fukuoka, Chuo-ku, Daimyo 2-9-5; Tel. 092-715-0731. See ECC description earlier. (JIJ).
* ELC; 880, Miyazaki, Miyata-cho 10-22, Eikaiwa Bldg. 2F; Tel. 0985-25-1565. 3 foreign teachers. Many types of classes. (JIJ).
* Hiroshima YMCA; 730, Hiroshima, Naka-ku, Hachobori 7-11; Tel. 082-228-2269. 9 foreign teachers. (JIJ).
* Kagoshima Foreign Language Center, Dai Ichi Seimei Bldg. Zenkan, 4-1 Oguro-cho, Kagoshima 892; Tel. 0992-23-6824. 3 foreign teachers. (JIJ).
* Kitakyushu YMCA; 802, Fukuoka-ken, Kitakyushu-shi, Kokura Kita-ku, Kaji-cho 2-3-13; Tel. 093-531-1587. 4 foreign teachers with variety of courses. (JIJ).
* Kumamoto YMCA; 860, Kumamoto, Shinmachi 1-3-8; Tel. 096-353-6391. 8 foreign teachers for general classes. (JIJ).

* Nihon Business School; 812, Fukuoka, Hakata Ekimae 4-18-6; Tel. 092-411-6423. 3 foreign teachers, mostly vocational English classes. (JIJ).

* Okinawa English Center; 900, Okinawa-ken, Naha-shi, Izumizaki 1-11-12; Tel. 0988-61-1487. 3 foreign instructor. Okinawa is an island about 500 miles from the mainland. (JIJ).

* Sato Business School, 2-4-10 Tenjin, Chuo-ku, Fukuoka 810; Tel. 771-8261. 4 foreign instructors. (JIJ).

* SDA; 730, Hiroshima, Naka-ku, Takeya-cho 4-8; Tel. 082-241-2464. All foreign teachers (4). (JIJ).

SAPPORO AREA AND NORTHERN JAPAN

* IAY; 060, Sapporo, Chuo-ku, Minami Ichijo 4-chome, Hinode Bldg.; Tel. 011-281-5188. 19 foreign teachers. Large school with wide variety of classes. (JIJ).

* Berlitz, Sapporo Bldg. 9F, Nihon Seimei, 4-1-1 Nishi, Kita Sanjo, Chuo-ku, Sapporo 060; Tel. 221-4701. All foreign teachers (11). See earlier description of Berlitz. (JIJ).

* English Circles/EC; 060, Sapporo, Chuo-ku, Minami Ichijo Nishi 5-chome, President Bldg. 3F; Tel. 011-221-0279. 10 foreign teachers in Sapporo's largest and oldest English school. (JIJ).

* James Eikaiwa; 980, Miyage-ken, Sendai-shi, Chuo 3-3-10, Chuo Sogo Bldg. 5F; Tel. 0222-67-4911. All foreign teachers (19) for general classes. (JIJ).

* New Day School; 980, Sendai-shi, Kokubu-cho 2-15-16, Company Bldg. 5F; Tel. 0222-65-4288. 16 foreign teachers specialize in children's classes. (JIJ).

* Nihon Business School; 001, Sapporo, Kita-ku, Kita Rokujo Nishi 6-chome; Tel. 011-717-7751. 4 foreign teachers. Emphasis on vocational English. (JIJ).

* Nihon Business Sogo Semmon Gakuin; 060, Sapporo, Chuo-ku, Odori Higashi 1, Odori Bus Center Bldg.; Tel. 011-241-8311. 5 foreign teacher. Vocational English classes mostly. (JIJ).

* Tohoku Gaikokugo Gakkoo, Chuo 4-2-25, Sendai-shi, Miagi-ken 980; Tel. 0222-67-3847. 13 foreign teachers emphasizes conversation for vocational training. (JIJ).